Let's Talk About Numbers

Let's Talk About Numbers

How the Letters of Your Name Coincide with the Law of Vibration and Your Life Situations

Patricia Kennedy and Nancy Gustin

Acknowledgments

We want to thank Louise Gartner for her boundless support and encouragement over the years and for her assistance in editing this book. We would never have accomplished this without you.

Contents

Preface

I am a Spiritualist minister and medium who has used numerology as a tool in my mediumship for over fifty years. As a past president of the Indiana Association of Spiritualists and a resident medium at Camp Chesterfield, Indiana, I've taught many mediumship and numerology classes over the years, and I've given thousands of readings to people from around the world.

During that time, I've had numerous requests to write a book that explains my system of numerology and how I use it as a tool in my mediumship. This book is in answer to those requests, but you don't need to be a medium to do numerology, so I devote little time and attention to aspects of mediumship in this book.

For readers who are mediums, please note that when I'm giving someone a reading, certain things in the chart will stand out for me. Spirit draws me to what needs to be said at the moment. You can take the book and learn from it, but you have to let Spirit step in and guide you. I give Spirit all the credit. I can look at your chart and look at it again in six months and tell you something different, because there will be things that you have changed to make it change. Your vibration brings the change. The Spirit world brings the change.

I hope this book provides you with useful information, and I trust that Spirit will bring whatever is in the highest and best interest of all involved.

--Patricia J. Kennedy

Chapter 1

Introduction to Numerology

What Is Numerology?

Numerology is the study of the significance of numbers on our lives based upon the vibrations associated with those numbers. Modern numerology as we know it in the Western world is attributed to Mrs. L. Dow Balliett. In her book *Vibration: How to Attain Success Through the Strength of Vibration: A System of Numbers as Taught by Pythagoras*, published in 1905, Balliett explains, "As we understand the teaching of the old master, all things are in a vibratory condition; the higher the rate of vibration the more spirit force an object contains and the more positive it is in its nature; the slower the rate of vibration, the less force it contains and the more negative it is in its action."

Balliett says she developed her system of numerology using the Bible and the works of Pythagoras, Plato, and other philosophers. She attributes the idea of energetic vibration of letters and numbers to Pythagoras. "Pythagoras says every letter of the alphabet has its own rate of vibration and color. He divided numbers in this way:

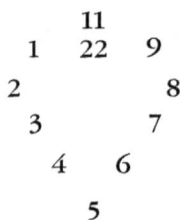

$$
\begin{array}{ccc}
 & 11 & \\
1 & 22 & 9 \\
2 & & 8 \\
3 & & 7 \\
4 & 6 & \\
 & 5 & \\
\end{array}
$$

into odd and even; into limited and unlimited, and gave the preference to odd numbers. But we consider all of them necessary." Each number also has its own rate of vibration.

Balliett divided the alphabet into nine parts, and assigned a number value to each letter, as follows:

1	2	3	4	5	6	7	8	9
A	B	C	D	E	F	G	H	I
J	K	L	M	N	O	P	Q	R
S	T	U	V	W	X	Y	Z	

By adding the number values of the letters in our names, we are able to determine the energetic vibration of our names. Balliett believed that many of life's problems have their solutions in understanding the vibration found in our names and birth numbers. She offered her system as a way to analyze the names of people, places, and things in our environments to determine those vibrating in harmony or disharmony with us. The system of numerology in this book uses the letter/number values as assigned by Balliett.

If we consider that most things in the universe have energy, her ideas make sense. Each color vibrates at a different frequency, and that allows us to distinguish between one color and another. Our bodies are comprised of cells that have molecules of hydrogen, oxygen, carbon, etc., and each of those molecules has protons and electrons that are spinning around a nucleus. Our cells are constantly in vibration.

In music, we understand that different notes on the scale vibrate at a different frequency. Higher pitched notes vibrate faster than lower pitched notes. Music also demonstrates how some frequencies can be compatible with others (harmony) while others are not (dissonance). Balliett understood the law of vibration, and she gave it practical application for our lives by offering us a system for determining the energetic vibration of our names and birth numbers.

Reverend Patricia J. Kennedy used Balliett's work as the foundation upon which she developed the numerology system described in this book. The information that follows stems from audio recordings and meetings with Reverend Kennedy that occurred over several years before her death in 2018 and is told from her perspective.

Numerology and Mediumship

I'm a numerologist, a medium, and an ordained Spiritualist minister. In this book, I'll be demonstrating how numbers can really talk to you. I've been doing numerology for more than fifty years, and I've done thousands of charts. While you don't have to be a medium to do numerology, as a medium, I use numerology as a tool during my readings.

When you are really tuned in as a medium, you're able to communicate with the so-called dead. When I do a reading, I do a Numerology Chart starting at the time of your life now. Numerology is a wonderful tool when you use it with Spirit, and by Spirit, I am referring to your spirit guides and loved ones who have made their transitions. Spirit provides guidance using numerology as an instrument. That is what Spirit has done for me all these years. Numerology helps me to tune in, and people get more with their readings when I use this tool. So, I don't do readings without the chart anymore.

It is important to mention that I believe in reincarnation and that we are re-born with karma. I believe we are put into people's lives for a reason. Keep this in mind as you read this book, because many of the key numbers and interpretations are based upon these beliefs.

Also important is how this book differs from other numerology books. Many systems of numerology exist. Although I have studied a number of different books on the subject over the years, the contents of this book are my own system, informed by my spirit guides. My system is not a defined system, because a number may have a different meaning depending on where it is in your chart, and I let Spirit decide. If I were doing a reading for you, even when I've read for you before, I would still do your chart again, because the chart is going to tell a different story each time. Spirit directs me when I do a reading. Even when I have done a chart before, I will see something new.

Chapter 2

Numerology Basics

In my system of numerology, I use your full name given at the time of birth and your date of birth to determine the following five key numbers: Soul Number, Identity Number, Impression Number, Birth Force Number, and Destiny Number. The first three (Soul, Identity, and Impression) numbers are derived from your name. The fourth (Birth Force) number is calculated from your date of birth. The fifth (Destiny) number is determined by adding the values of the name and birthdate.

The Soul Number is derived from the vowels in your name. In addition to *A*, *E*, *I*, *O*, and *U*, I consider the letter *Y* to be a vowel. Numerologists differ in their use of *Y* as a vowel, but I always consider it to be a vowel. The Soul Number provides information about your past lives.

The Identity Number comes from the consonants in your name, and it reflects what you present to the world.

The Impression Number is calculated from your whole name, including the vowels and the consonants. Just like it sounds, the Impression Number reflects the impression others have of you, and it includes the things in your personality that you may not be aware of yourself. We all have blind spots, and sometimes others see things in us that we don't see in ourselves.

From your birthdate, I determine your Birth Force Number. The Birth Force Number gives a glimpse into the kinds of people, places, opportunities, and challenges that will cross your path in this lifetime.

The last of the key numbers is the Destiny Number. The Destiny Number is found by adding your birth name (Impression Number) and your birthdate (Birth Force Number). The Destiny Number tells me your direction in life.

As I mentioned, I believe in karma; and I believe you bring into your current incarnation unresolved issues, unpaid debts, and aspirations from your past lives. You may or may not be aware of these issues. While this may sound negative, it doesn't need to be. Unresolved issues, unpaid debts, and aspirations from previous lives present opportunities for growth in your current incarnation. Working on karma is necessary for your soul's evolution.

Your karmic lessons represent the areas your soul has chosen to work on in this incarnation, and they are determined from the numbers that are missing from your name. I will explain this further in Chapter 4 when I talk about the Inclusion.

Karmic debts, on the other hand, represent some abuse of power, work, love, or freedom in your previous incarnation, and those debts must be re-paid. Let's face it. As humans, sometimes our emotions get the better of us, and we act selfishly from feelings of fear, anger, or even hate rather than acting from love. You may or may not have karmic debts. If you do, it will show in your numbers. The Karmic Numbers are 10, 13, 14, 16, and 19. I will explain what these numbers represent in Chapter 3.

Whether or not you have karmic debts to repay in this incarnation, remember that you choose your actions. Regardless of the emotions you feel in the situation, you can still choose to act from a place of love and what is in the highest and best interest of all involved. Your actions in this incarnation will affect your karma in your next incarnation. So, keep this in mind.

In addition to Karmic Numbers, your key numbers may include Master Numbers. Master Numbers contain powerful energy and potential, making them aspirational in nature. The Master Numbers are the double-digit numbers 11, 22, 33, 44, 55, 66, 77, 88, and 99, with the numbers 11, 22, and 33 being the most common. As human consciousness evolves, we will begin to feel the higher vibrations associated with Master Numbers 44 and beyond; but, for now, they are still rare, so I will not address them in this book. I will explain more about Master Numbers in Chapter 3.

Regardless of your numbers, numerology can shed light on the issues you have chosen to work on in this incarnation, and this can be immensely helpful.

Number Values for Each Letter

I use the same number values for each letter that Balliett attributed to Pythagoras. Here is the chart of number values for each letter again for your reference.

1	2	3	4	5	6	7	8	9
A	B	C	D	E	F	G	H	I
J	K	L	M	N	O	P	Q	R
S	T	U	V	W	X	Y	Z	

How Numbers Are Added in Numerology

As you can see from the letter/number chart, each letter has a number associated with it. To determine the values in a word or name, you put each number with the associated letter and add across. Then, you reduce any double-digit numbers to a single digit by adding them together. To make it easier for me, I put the numbers associated with the vowels above the letters, and the numbers associated with the consonants below them. For example, see the word HEAVEN below:

$$
\begin{array}{ll}
5\ 1\ \ 5 & = 5+1+5=11 \\
\text{HEAVEN} & \\
8\ \ \ \ 4\ \ 5 & = 8+4+5=17
\end{array}
$$

Now, I would add 11+17 = 28. Then add 2+8 = 10. Then add 1+0 = 1. So, the shorthand way of writing this would be 28/10/1.

Now, let's look at the word HELL.

$$
\begin{array}{ll}
5 & = 5 \\
\text{HELL} & \\
8 \quad 33 & = 8+3+3 = 14
\end{array}
$$

Now, I would add 5+14 = 19. Then add 1+9 = 10. Then add 1+0 = 1. So, the shorthand way of writing this would be 19/10/1.

This may be a good time to talk about the power of words and their associated numbers. Although both words ultimately reduce to the number 1, there are differences in the power and meaning of these words, and most people would agree that heaven and hell are not the same things.

As a Spiritualist, I don't believe that heaven and hell are physical places. I believe they are states of consciousness. To me, the 28/10/1 represents heaven or the higher consciousness, whereas the 19/10/1 represents hell or the lower consciousness. So, if a word or name adds to a 28/10/1, I would leave it written as a 28/10/1. If it adds to a 19/10/1, I would leave it written as a 19/10/1.

If this seems confusing, don't worry. It will make more sense when we discuss the characteristics of numbers in Chapter 3. The 28/10/1 and 19/10/1 are special numbers that we call Karmic Numbers. For now, I just want you to focus on how to put the numbers with each letters, how to add them and reduce them to get a single digit, and how to write the shorthand version of this process, as we did with the examples above (i.e., 28/10/1 and 19/10/1). We will discuss interpretations later.

In studying the work of many different Numerologists, one of the things I noticed and often found confusing was the different ways in which numbers were added. For example, one Numerologist would add all the way across and then reduce. Another Numerologist would add the letters in the first name and reduce those, then go to the middle name and add and reduce, then go to the last name and add and reduce. Then, finally, would add the reduced numbers of each name together to get a final number.

Most of the time, the method you use to add the letter values doesn't matter, because you will end up with the same reduced number in the end. However, occasionally it does matter, and you may miss a Master Number or a Karmic Number in a name because of the method you used. Let me use John F. Kennedy's name as an example to illustrate what I mean.

To calculate JFK's Soul Number, I will add and reduce just the vowels in his name.

$$15/6 \qquad 17/8$$
$$6 \qquad 9 + 5{+}1 \qquad 5 + 5{+}7$$
John Fitzgerald Kennedy

When adding and reducing each name separately first and then adding them together, we get 6 + 6 + 8 = 20, and 2+0 = 2.

However, if we add his name all the way across first, and then reduce, we get 6 + 15 + 17 = 38, and 3 + 8 = 11, which is a Master Number. So, you may want to add both ways just to see if one way of adding yields a Master Number or Karmic Number.

I still reduce Master Numbers and Karmic Numbers down to a single digit, but I leave the Master or Karmic Number there to call my attention to it. For example, I would write the Master Number 11 as 11/2 and the Karmic Number 19 as 19/10/1.

Chapter 3

Number Characteristics

Each number has certain characteristics (positive and negative) based on its inherent vibration. A number will have a different meaning depending on where it is in your chart. I will explain this more in depth later in the book.

Number 1 – Leadership, Beginnings

Positive Characteristics

Independent	Initiative
Self-sufficient	Action-oriented
Ambitious	Goal directed
Unique	Originality
Confident	Powerful
Determined	Beginnings
Leadership	

Negative Characteristics

Egotistical	Aggressive
Impatient	Impulsive
Opinionated	Dominating
Know-it-all	Boastful
Selfish	Cynical
Self-centered	Hermit
Forceful	Intolerant
Pushy	Leaving things unfinished

Number 2 – Partnership, Diplomacy

Positive Characteristics

Supportive	Intuitive
Loving	Sensitive
Receptive	Gentle
Patient	Calm
Cooperative	Kind
Subtle	Relationship oriented
Adaptable	Diplomacy
Peaceful	Peacemaker
Harmonious	Balance
Gracious	Considerate
Understanding	Tolerant
Persuasive	Parental
Follower	Partnerships
Unity	Duality

Negative Characteristics

Passive	Self-conscious
Vacillating	Self-sacrificing
Indecisive	Lacking in self-confidence
Deceitful	Hypersensitive
Fearful	Nitpicky
Shy	Possessive
Timid	Weak

Number 3 – Creativity, Self-expression

Positive Characteristics

Creative	Dramatic
Clever	Excitable
Joyful	Emotional
Happy	Spontaneous
Humorous	Versatile
Expressive	Warm
Tasteful	Generous
Original	Playful
Talented	Inspirational
Enthusiastic	Pleasure-seeking
Energetic	Youthful
Entertaining	Quick witted
Imaginative	Sociable
Artistic	Trinity

Negative Characteristics

Extravagant	Lazy
Hyper	Outspoken
Superficial	Impulsive
Chaotic	Moody
Frivolous	Flirtatious
Disorganized	Exaggerative
Self-centered	Wasteful
Talkative	Unforgiving
Scattered	Self-indulgent
Insincere	Impractical

Number 4 – Work, Organization, Industry

Positive Characteristics

Practical	Dedicated
Industrious	Thoughtful
Disciplined	Trustworthy
Patient	Respectable
Traditional	Reliable
Devoted	Efficient
Hard working	Organized
Serious	Predictable
Stable	Orderly
Calm	Consistent
Conventional	Responsible
Honest	Conscientious
Faithful	Determined
Cautious	

Negative Characteristics

Narrow	Stubborn
Controlling	Argumentative
Rigid	Suspicious
Inflexible	Boring
Joyless	

Number 5 – Change

Positive Characteristics

Versatile	Risk taker
Changeable	Affectionate
Clever	Stimulating
Resourceful	Open
Self-sufficient	Progressive
Understanding	Freedom loving
Exciting	Curious
Fascinating	Loving
Adventurous	Pleasure-seeking

Negative Characteristics

Irresponsible	Critical/Hurtful
Undisciplined	Scattered
Impulsive	Hasty
Impatient	Quick tempered
Gambler	Restless
Dissatisfied	Rebellious
Discontent	Moody
Nervous	Unstable

Number 6 – Family, Responsibility, Service

Positive Characteristics

Family	Loyal
Responsibility	Healer
Marriage	Nurturing
Committed relationships	Caretaking
Generous	Protective
Responsible	Family-oriented
Supportive	Service-oriented
Self-sacrificing	Humanitarian
Honest	Understanding
Kind	Unselfish
Reliable	Committed
Sympathetic	Spiritually protected
Devoted	Open-minded

Negative Characteristics

Anxious	Interfering
Worrier	Dominating
Unrealistic	Selfish
Unreasonable	Demanding
Fussy	Overprotective
Opinionated	Smothering
Outspoken	Unforgiving
Complainer	People-pleasing
Stubborn	Approval seeking

Number 7- Thinker, Philosopher, Mystic

Positive Characteristics

Analytical	Solitary
Intellectual	Loner
Studious	Secretive
Spiritual	Private
Metaphysical	Intuitive
Philosophical	Quiet
Peaceful	Scholarly
Faithful	Understanding
Mystical	Wise
Meditative	Introverted

Negative Characteristics

Cold	Suspicious/skeptical
Unreasonable	Lazy
Sarcastic	Dreamy
Aloof/distant	Prideful
Reserved	Eccentric
Moody	Perfectionistic
Bitter	Unsociable

Number 8 – Achievement, Success, Money

Positive Characteristics

Successful	Authority/Power
Ambitious	Trustworthy
Efficient	Devoted
Orderly	Supervising/Directing/Leading
Adaptable	Strong
Self-reliant	Goal-directed
Self-controlled	Money/wealth
Tough	Business
Wise	Government
Capable	Problem-solver
Courageous	Dependable
Fair	Achievement
Focused	Organization
Thorough	Integrity

Negative Characteristics

Materialistic	Guilt-ridden
Hard	Tense
Stubborn	Money problems
Jealous	Impatient
Insecure	Workaholic
Controlling	Egotistical
Moody	Attention-seeking

Number 9 – Humanitarian, Completions

Positive Characteristics

Compassionate	Romantic
Humanitarian	Courageous
Selfless	Fortunate
Dramatic	Inspirational
Forgiving	Spiritual
Intuitive	Religious
Charitable	Understanding
Successful	Accepting
Sympathetic	Endings/completions

Negative Characteristics

Emotional	Self-centered
Idealistic	Selfish
Impractical	Impulsive
Dissatisfied	Impatient
Deceptive	Possessive
Conceited	Moody
Restless	Approval-seeking

Master Number 11 – Spiritual Messenger

Positive Characteristics

Dreamer	Spiritual teacher
Humanitarian	Inspirational
Leader	Energetic
Mystic	Intense
Perceptive	Talented
Prophetic	Sensitive
Visionary	Influential
Spiritual	Peacemaker
Seeker	

Negative Characteristics

Cold	Fearful
Detached	Attention-seeking
Infamous	Shy
Intolerant	Unfeeling
Uncaring	Distant
Nervous	Secretive

Number 22 – Master Builder

Positive Characteristics

Powerful	Honest
Intuitive	Leader
Competent	Productive
Directing	Hard-working
Master organizer/planner/builder	Disciplined
Courageous	Understanding
Confident	Visionary
Ambitious	Spiritual
Creative	Mystical/Occult

Negative Characteristics

Self-promoting
Workaholic
Boastful

Master Number 33 – Master Teacher

Positive Characteristics

Kind	Wise
Compassionate	Generous
Altruistic	Outgoing
Loving	Forgiving
Dutiful	Guiding
Ministering	Visionary
Nurturing	Selfless
Service to others	Self-sacrificing
Healing	Avatar
Reformer	Humanitarian

Negative Characteristics

Emotional
Pushy
Intolerant
Rigid
Overprotective
Self-righteous
Self-destructive
Attention seeking
Martyr

Master Numbers

I mentioned that Master Numbers contain powerful energy and potential, making them aspirational in nature. Let me explain what I mean by that. Master Numbers are associated with higher spiritual matters involving service to mankind. They are an indication of your highest potential or purpose in this life. The area of that potential depends on where the Master Number falls in your name or birthdate. To be clear, having a Master Number in your name or birthdate doesn't make you a master at something. In fact, you may have to work even harder in that area to realize your true potential.

When I'm doing a reading, I have no way of knowing whether or not someone is living up to their highest potential, so I let Spirit decide. Spirit will guide me to either keep the number as a Master Number or to reduce it to a single digit. There are times when I need to reduce a Master Number, such as when I'm determining a person's Pinnacles and Challenges as described in Chapter 7.

When I do a person's chart, I will write the Master Numbers as 11/2, 22/4, or 33/6 rather than reducing and just going with the 2, 4, or 6, because seeing the Master Number provides me with information. For example, the number 29/11/2 gives me the impression that the person is working in the light, becoming enlightened, or being protected by Spirit, depending on where the 29/11/2 is in their numbers.

If 29/11/2 is their Soul Number (see Chapter 4), the person worked in the light in a past life. If they were born on the 29th, the person is protected by Spirit. When I see an 11/2 Essence Number in the chart (I explain Essence Numbers in Chapter 9), it tells me the person is trying to grow spiritually at that time.

Karmic Numbers

The Karmic Numbers are 10, 13, 14, 16, and 19. Karma is akin to the idea of reaping what you sow. In your current incarnation, these numbers suggest opportunities to repay karmic debts or to learn karmic lessons. Karmic debts suggest a misuse of work, freedom, love, or power in your previous incarnations. Karmic lessons, on the other hand, are lessons you did not deal with in a past life, either because you avoided them for some reason or because the opportunities never presented themselves to you.

You can determine your karmic lessons by finding what numbers are missing from your name. I will explain this more fully in the next chapter. Karmic debts have more to do with selfishness and mistreatment of others in a previous incarnation. The 1 at the beginning of each of these numbers represents selfishness or self-centeredness in the way that you approached the issue of work, freedom, love, or power.

If one of your key numbers is a 13, 14, 16, or 19, you may have a karmic debt to repay from a past life. Don't let these numbers scare you. It doesn't mean you are cursed. Trust that all is in Divine order. While dealing with karmic debt may present challenges for you in this incarnation, it is necessary for your soul's growth. Remember that you are responsible for your actions. So, understanding the meanings of these numbers can help you to know what the underlying principles are that you need to address. In other words, in this incarnation, you can choose to take the feelings and needs of others into consideration and act responsibly.

The number 10 is the only Karmic Number that is considered positive, but it has the potential to be negative as well. The number 10 is not associated with a karmic debt. See below for a quick reference of the meanings of the Karmic Numbers.

Number 10: I refer to 10/1 as the God Force number. Heaven adds to 28/10/1. The number 10 is associated with rebirth. However, in the negative, it can be associated with starting things but leaving them unfinished.

Number 13: The lesson of the 13/4 is to apply yourself and to do your fair share of work, as 4 is the number for work. The 13/4 challenges you to deal with change and to be efficient. When it surfaces in the numerology chart, 13/4 indicates a time of change of friendships, relationships, home, or job.

Number 14: With 14/5, a person would be drawn to the lower self. The lesson of the 14/5 is to learn moderation and to not go to extremes.

Number 16: The lesson of the 16/7 is to cope with losses, to understand the cycle of destruction and rebuilding of your life, and to learn the spiritual truths involving willpower and what is right.

Number 19: The lesson of the 19/10/1 is the proper use of power in this lifetime. In other words, it involves standing up for yourself but not being domineering.

Later in this book, I will show you how to set up and read a numerology chart. The chart gives a snapshot of what a person may be experiencing during a particular time in their life. When I see Karmic Numbers in someone's chart, I know they are facing some challenges at that particular time. Each Karmic Number presents its own challenges. I'll explain this more fully when I teach you how to read a numerology chart. For now, just familiarize yourself with the Karmic Numbers, so you'll recognize them when finding your own or someone else's numbers.

Chapter 4

The Importance of the Name

Your full name given at the time of birth reveals a lot of information about you. From your name alone, I can derive your Soul Number, Identity Number, and Impression Number. The Soul Number (vowels) provides information about your past lives. Your character, learning, experiences, and actions incurring any karmic debts in your previous lives will determine the lessons you have come here to learn in this incarnation. The Identity Number (consonants) reflects what you present to the world. The Impression Number (vowels + consonants) reflects the impression others have of you.

Your name influences where you choose to live. You can work the numbers for your cities, your addresses, your phone numbers, what you name your children, your business, etc. I believe you choose your own name before you are ever born. You know what you have agreed to coming into this lifetime.

A lot of old souls are incarnating now. If you look at the charts of Indigo children and Rainbow children, you will realize that these kids have come to teach us. We're not teaching them at all. I would encourage you to do the charts of people in your family. If you do, you'll know more about them, why they did things, or what they may have been going through at certain times in their lives.

For purposes of the numerology chart, each of your names (first name, middle name, last name) represents a different aspect of you. For example, the first name represents the physical aspect. The middle name represents the mental, emotional, and occupational aspects. And the last name represents the spiritual aspect. If you have multiple middle names, separate them into their respective parts as follows:

First Name = Physical Name
Second Name = Mental Name
Third Name = Emotional Name
Fourth Name = Professional/Occupational Name
Last Name = Spiritual Name

The Inclusion List

The Inclusions are the numbers in your name, for example, how many 1s, 2s, 3s…9s you have in your name after you have assigned number values to each of the letters in your name. Look at your entire name given at birth, and count the number of letters that equal 1 (A, J, S), then 2 (B, K, T), then 3 (C, L, U) and so on to determine what numbers are either missing or are in abundance. Numbers that are missing represent karmic lessons that you have come here to learn, whereas an overabundance of a certain number (4 or more of that number) represents an imbalance in that area.

If your name includes every number (nothing is missing), it means you are an old soul. An old soul is someone who has been around many times and whose soul is saying, "Give it all to me this lifetime. I want to work on everything." If you aren't missing any numbers, and all of your numbers are balanced, you can wear the hats of many people. The numbers I like to see balanced are the 1, 5, and 9. When looking at a person's Inclusion List, if I see three or four numbers missing, it tells me the person is naïve and has a lot to learn. They sometimes trust so much that they don't always think for themselves. They can be easily manipulated.

Below is an example of an Inclusion List for someone who is missing 3 numbers.

1s = 4 (Overabundance of 1s suggests someone who can be egotistical, impatient, and domineering. The person is independent, wants to be in charge, and initiates but may leave things unfinished)

2s = 2 (More than one serious relationship. Working on partnerships and relationships.)

3s = 1 (Expression, creativity)

4s = 0 (The 4 karmic lesson is to learn to be organized and to work to establish a solid foundation in life.)

5s = 4 (The overabundance suggests spreading oneself too thin)

6s = 0 (The person's spirit didn't choose to have children in this lifetime. That doesn't mean the person wouldn't have had children. It could mean a miscarriage, abortion, raising someone else's children, not being able to raise the children the way the person wanted, teaching children, or working around children. The 6 karmic lesson has to do with family matters, responsibility, and with healing as well.)

7s = 1 (Analytical, intellectual, spiritual/religious, introspective, private)

8s = 0 (One of the biggest challenges. Material things are not that important to this person. Having no 8s suggests someone who makes money but can spend it. The 8 karmic lesson involves learning to manage one's own finances and affairs.)

9s = 2 (Humanitarian)

Number 1: In all the years that I've done numerology readings, I've met very few people who were missing the number 1. If the person has no 1s, he or she is an angel walking among you who will never have an ego. One is ego. Some people have five or six 1s. They don't know how to shut their minds off. It's mental, mental, mental, ego, ego, ego. People who are missing the number 1 need to learn how to make their own decisions.

Number 2: If missing the number 2, it shows me the person's spirit did not choose to be married in this lifetime. Rather, they have come here to work on partnerships and relationships. An overabundance can indicate a male with more female energy or a female with more male energy. If I was giving a reading to a female I didn't know, I might say something like, "It shows me you have a lot of male tendencies. Do you know that we are made up of masculine and feminine? So, you would want to be one who is so independent and controlling that you would have to look at how you utilize that type of energy." However, if I was giving a reading to a male I didn't know, and I saw many 2s, I would say the opposite, "I see here that you have a lot of feminine energies." When giving a reading, I don't say *married*. I say *relationships* and discuss how they are dealing with relationships. I would say, "Partnerships are something you have to work at, because it is hard for you to find someone who will walk beside you. You tend to have someone who is trying to control you or who you would follow." You have to watch how you say it. It helps open the doors to what you're really saying. If they have a question about relationships, you may ask, "Would you like to share with me the name of your partner, so we can see what is going on between the two of you?"

Number 3: People missing the number 3 need to learn how to express themselves. People with many 3s in their name tend to be artistic, creative, and free spirited. They often become writers, actors, entertainers, or tend to be very crafty.

Number 4: People missing the number 4 are not organized, and they likely dislike work, as 4 is associated with work. They will need to learn to be organized and to work diligently to lay a solid foundation for their lives. An overabundance of 4s suggests a tendency to get too caught up in the details or to take on too many tasks.

Number 5: People who are missing the number 5 need to learn to accept and deal with change. People with an overabundance of 5s tend to spread themselves too thin, have too many interests, too many changes, and a tendency to misuse their freedom.

Number 6: People missing the number 6 will have lessons involving family, healing, and learning to accept responsibility. No 6s can be an indication that their spirit has chosen not to have children. It doesn't mean they won't have children. It could mean they will work with children and help them. It could mean that family is something they had to learn about in this lifetime. It can also mean healing. People with an overabundance of 6s may be overly responsible and concerned about family, and self-sacrificing to the point of becoming martyrs.

Number 7: People missing the number 7 need to learn to go within, to become introspective and to listen to their inner voice to find their answers. They may have lessons involving spirituality or religion.

Number 8: People missing the number 8 have lessons to learn around financial matters and managing their lives. They may make money, but they won't keep it. Material things will not be that important to them. There may also be lessons involving power and authority when 8s are missing or are in abundance. People with 8s may own their own businesses at some point in their lives or be professionals. If they have an overabundance of 8s, they may be too materialistic or power hungry.

Number 9: People missing 9s have to learn unconditional love and forgiveness. People with an overabundance of 9s may be so devoted to their humanitarian missions that they forsake their own needs or the needs of their family.

Importance of the Vowels

Some Numerologists discuss the significance of the first vowel in the first name. The first vowel is significant, but not in a reading. People who are coming to me for a reading are coming for guidance, and they don't really want to hear about their personality characteristics. To me, the vowels are a past life issue. So, I am less concerned with what the first vowel is in the name than I am with the total of the vowels in the first, middle, and last names and total of all the vowels combined.

The vowels represent what you are bringing in from your past life into your current incarnation and provide me with information about some of the issues you may be addressing in this lifetime. When associating the numbers with each letter, I put the numbers for the vowels above the name, and the numbers for the consonants below the name. This makes it easier to calculate the Soul and Identity Numbers. As mentioned earlier, I consider the vowels to be *A, E, I, O, U,* and *Y.* Numerologists vary in their use of *Y* as a vowel, but I always consider *Y* a vowel.

The vowels are also important when it comes to the numerology chart. The vowels will mean different things depending on which of your names they are in. For example, your first name represents your physical aspects. Your middle name represents your mental/emotional/occupational aspects. And your last name represents your spiritual aspects. So, if I see an *E* (E = 5, 5 is the number of change), and it is in your first name (physical name), it means physical changes (such as a move). If the *E* is on your middle name (mental/emotional/occupational name), it would suggest a job change or a change that is affecting you emotionally. If the *E* is on your last name (spiritual name), it suggests change of a spiritual nature.

I will explain this in depth when I show you how to set up and read a numerology chart in Chapter 9. If the vowels on your physical name add to the same number as the vowels on your mental/emotional/occupational or spiritual names, it means you had a lot of balance in your past life, because these are balanced.

Key Numbers Derived from the Name

The three key numbers derived from the name are the Soul Number, the Identity Number, and the Impression Number. To illustrate how to calculate each of these numbers, I will use John Fitzgerald Kennedy as an example.

Soul Number

The Soul Number represents your past life. In other words, the Soul Number tells you what your soul brought into this life from your past life. It is important to understand what you are bringing into your current incarnation from your past life in terms of your character or past learning for a couple of reasons. First, it helps you to better understand yourself in terms of what may be influencing your motivations, desires, fears, values, and behaviors. For this reason, the Soul Number, more than any other key number, represents the *why* of your life. Second, it provides useful information in understanding any karmic debts you may have incurred from abusing your power or engaging in wrongdoing in your previous life. Understanding your karmic debts affords you the insight to recognize opportunities to learn those lessons and to re-pay past debts.

To find the Soul Number, add the values of the vowels (A, E, I, O, U, and Y) in the name and reduce until you get a single digit. Let's start by writing the values for each vowel above JFK's name. See my example on the next page.

6   9   5 1   5 5 7

John Fitzgerald Kennedy

Now add the values and reduce until you get a single digit, as follows: 6 + 9 + 5 + 1 + 5 + 5 + 7 = 38, 3+8 = 11, 1 + 1 = 2. Since JFK's Soul Number includes a Master Number (11), we would write his Soul Number as 11/2.

If your Soul Number is one of the universal numbers (1-9), you can refer to the basic characteristics of that number in Chapter 3 to better understand what learning, wisdom, or character traits from your past life are influencing you in your current incarnation. I have additions to those characteristics below.

Remember to look for Master Numbers (11, 22, 33) and Karmic Numbers (10, 13, 14, 16, 19) when determining your Soul Number. As a reminder, if your Soul Number is a Master Number or Karmic Number, it will have special significance, and you will want to keep the Master or Karmic Number along with the reduction when you write the Soul Number. I will elaborate on each of the Master or Karmic Soul Numbers along with the meanings for the universal Soul Numbers below, but first, let's find your Soul Number.

Find your Soul Number now by writing out your full name given at birth and putting the associated number above each vowel in your name.

_____   _____   _____
First name   Middle name   Last name

If you have more than one middle name, remember to include those too. Now, put the number associated with each vowel above it.

As a reminder, the vowels have the following number values:

A = 1
E = 5
I = 9
O = 6
U = 3
Y = 7

Now, add the values and reduce until you get a single digit. Do you have any Master Numbers (11, 22, 33) or Karmic Numbers (10, 13, 14, 16, 19)? Once you've determined your Soul Number, refer to the meanings listed below to learn what your soul has brought into this incarnation from your previous life.

Soul Number 1: If your Soul Number is 1, you were likely in a position of leadership or control over others in your previous life. As a result, you may still find that you don't like being in a subordinate position or being told what to do.

Karmic Soul Number 10/1: I consider 10/1 to be the God Force number. Whenever I see the 28/10/1 (HEAVEN adds to 28/10/1), it tells me you were working in the energy of what is called the higher self in your past life.

Karmic Soul Number 19/10/1: When I see the 19/10/1, I think of it as the Jewish sign. It tells me you were likely Jewish and went through the Holocaust and have been reincarnated from it. The value of hell is 19/10/1, and during the holocaust, the Jewish people went through hell. While the 19/10/1 Soul Number does not always mean that you were Jewish and went through the Holocaust (I let Spirit guide me about this), it is an indication that your soul is trying to raise from a hellish past life into the more spiritual, higher self in this life.

Soul Number 2: If you have a 2 Soul Number, you were a peacekeeper in your previous life. Peace, balance, and harmony were very important to you, for 2s dislike conflict. As a result, you are bringing tact, diplomacy, and the ability to negotiate into your current incarnation. You will seek a partnership, companionship, and/or marriage in which you can be in a supportive role, but it will be important for you to take care of yourself in the process and not let others walk all over you.

Soul Number 3: If your Soul Number is a 3, you were likely very creative and talented in your past life, for 3 is the number of self-expression. You may have been an artist, writer, musician, singer, dancer, or some other type of entertainer. Socializing and having fun were important to you. A 12/3 Soul Number is an indication that you were a free spirit in a past life. A 21/3, on the other hand, is an indication that you felt restricted, like your hands were tied. Perhaps you were unable to use your talents to express yourself as you would have liked.

Soul Number 4: If your Soul Number is a 4, you were organized, methodical, and a hard worker in your past life. You will have a tendency to be practical, dependable, and hardworking in your current incarnation. It will be important for you to balance work and play.

Karmic Soul Number 13/4: The 13/4 Soul Number tells me that you died of a man-made death. In other words, when you left your past life, you may have been murdered, smothered to death, burned alive, or you could have committed suicide.

Soul Number 5: A 5 Soul Number signifies that freedom was of utmost importance to you in your past life. You yearned for stimulation, variety, travel, and constant change.

Karmic Soul Number 14/5: If your Soul Number is a 14/5, you were one who taught or spoke of God in your past life.

Soul Number 6: Family and home were very important to you in your past life. You likely tend to be understanding, responsible, and family-oriented in your current incarnation.

Soul Number 7: You may have been a priest or a hermit in your past life. As a result, in this incarnation, you likely need alone time to think, read, or meditate.

Karmic Soul Number 16/7: A 16/7 Soul Number indicates that you may have abused love in your past life, and that you possibly hurt others as a result. You may have cheated on your spouse or acted irresponsibly in some manner and failed to honor your commitment.

Soul Number 8: In your past life, you were concerned with power, money, and success. You may have been a business tycoon or banker.

Soul Number 9: You were likely a humanitarian, philanthropist, minister, or doctor in your past life.

Soul Number 11: You were a free spirit, and you worked in the light in a past life. You were born in the light.

Soul Number 22: You envisioned and manifested projects that benefitted humanity in some large-scale way in your past life.

Soul Number 33: You served humanity as a teacher of unconditional love to guide people toward enlightenment or healing.

Identity Number

The Identity Number is determined by adding the values of all the consonants in your name and reducing to get a single digit. By identity, I mean how you see yourself, and what you think you are this lifetime. What you came into this lifetime thinking you were going to do professionally, spiritually, etc. Who are you? What are you? What choices you might be making in this lifetime.

Once you find your Identity Number, refer to the list below for the characteristics associated with your number. But first, let's look at an example.

John	Fitzgerald	Kennedy
1 85	6 287 9 34	2 55 4
1+8+5 = 14	6+2+8+7+9+3+4 = 39	2+5+5+4 = 16

Now, reduce each name separately and add them together. For example, the consonants in John = 14 (1+4) = 5. The consonants in Fitzgerald = 39 (3+9) = 12 (1+2) = 3. The consonants in Kennedy = 16 (1+6) = 7. Then add the reduced value of each name together. So, 5 + 3 + 7 = 15 (1+5) = 6. John Fitzgerald Kennedy's Identity Number is a 15/6. I consider 15/6 to be a number of detachment and the healing aspects of life.

Now, add up all the consonants in your name and reduce to a single digit, unless your consonants add to one of the Master Numbers (11, 22, or 33). The Karmic Numbers (10, 13, 14, 16, or 19) aren't as important to the Identity Number as they are to the Soul Number, so I reduce them to single digits and use the general meanings of the numbers 1 through 9.

Find your Identity Number now by writing out your full name given at birth and putting the associated number below each consonant in your name.

_____   _____   _____
    First name   **Middle name**   **Last name**

Remember to include all of your names. Here is the chart again to make it easier.

1	2	3	4	5	6	7	8	9
A	B	C	D	E	F	G	H	I
J	K	L	M	N	O	P	Q	R
S	T	U	V	W	X	Y	Z	

Now, add and reduce the values of the consonants until you get a single digit (unless you have a Master Number), and refer to the list below to see the predominant characteristics of that number. You can always refer to Chapter 3 for more in-depth information about each number. You may identify with some but not all of the characteristics of that number. That is to be expected.

Identity Number 1: Leader

Identity Number 2: Partner, diplomat, peacemaker

Identity Number 3: Artist, entertainer

Identity Number 4: Hard worker, organizer

Identity Number 5: Adventurer, risk taker

Identity Number 6: Parental, family-oriented, service work

Identity Number 7: Thinker, philosopher

Identity Number 8: Business, finance, government

Identity Number 9: Humanitarian, philanthropist

Identity Number 11: Mystic, spiritual messenger

Identity Number 22: Master planner, organizer, builder

Identity Number 33: Master teacher

Impression Number

Your Impression Number reveals the impression you give others, and that is not necessarily how you would like others to view you. It represents your true self, because it includes your Identity Number (who you think you are) and your Soul Number (what you brought in from your past lives). Your soul is driving your actions, and it is going to come out one way or another, even though you may not be aware of it.

You can find your Impression Number by adding the Soul Number (the vowels of the name) and the Identity Number (the consonants of the name), and then reducing until you get a single digit. Let's look at our JFK example to find his Impression Number. From our previous calculations, we learned that John Fitzgerald Kennedy's Soul Number is 11/2 and that his Identity Number is 15/6. When we add those together, we get his Impression Number (26/8).

11/2 (Soul Number)
+ 15/6 (Identity Number)

26/8 (Impression Number)

The number 8 is associated with business, government, power, wealth, ambition, and success. Eights are quite capable supervisors, directors, and leaders. Eights give the impression of being strong, visionary, goal-directed, and high achievers.

Now, you can find your Impression Number by adding together the values of your Soul and Identity Numbers and reducing to a single digit, unless your numbers add to the Master Numbers 11, 22, or 33.

_____ (Soul Number) + _____ (Identity Number) = _____ (Impression Number)

Once you have found your Impression Number, refer to Chapter 3 to find the characteristics of that number. Keep in mind that the impressions others have of you may be positive in some regards and negative in others. For example, if your Impression Number is 1, you may think you give the impression of being a natural leader who takes initiative, is ambitious, confident, and determined, but others may see you as a know-it-all who is forceful, pushy, aggressive, and dominating. So, read the positive and negative aspects of that number and consider what may be true for you. If you exhibit some of the negative characteristics of that number, it is never too late to make positive changes. The healthier you are physically, psychologically, and spiritually, the more likely you will be to espouse the positive characteristics of your numbers.

Chapter 5

The Importance of the Birthdate

Birth Force Number

The Birth Force Number represents your life path, or the *what* your higher self wants to accomplish in this lifetime. When you reincarnate, you start a whole new path. To find your Birth Force Number, add the month, day, and year of your birth.

Let's determine John F. Kennedy's Birth Force Number. His birthdate was 5-29-1917. When we add the month, day, and year of his birth, we get 5 + 29/11 + 18/9 = 5 + 11 + 9 = 25/7. So, his Birth Force

Number is a 7. A 7 Birth Force is the number of mystics, psychics, and those who want to develop their intellectual and analytical skills to gain knowledge, wisdom, and understanding in this incarnation.

Now, find your Birth Force Number by adding the month, day, and year of your birth and reducing to a single digit. Remember to look for Master Numbers. Once you've found your Birth Force Number, refer to the list of meanings below or revisit Chapter 3.

Birth Month	+	Birth Day	+	Birth Year	=	Birth Force Number

Birth Force Number 1: The number of the creator. The path of the 1 Birth Force involves independence and self-determination, using creativity to generate unique ideas and to initiate new ventures.

Birth Force Number 2: The path of the 2 Birth Force involves partnerships and relationships. The 2 Birth Force is relationship oriented, seeking to be supportive, cooperative, and diplomatic.

Birth Force Number 3: The path of the 3 Birth Force involves creativity and self-expression. Whether as an artist, actor, writer, musician, or entertainer, the 3 Birth Force will not be happy unless it is pursuing its talents as a way of expressing itself.

Birth Force Number 4: The path of the 4 Birth Force involves being practical, organized, disciplined, and responsible. The 4 Birth Force is traditional, doing things the conventional way. The path involves hard work, but the 4 will be consistent and persevere to lay the necessary groundwork for his/her life.

Birth Force Number 5: The path of the 5 Birth Force involves freedom, excitement, adventure, and change.

Birth Force Number 6: The path of the 6 Birth Force involves caretaking, so the 6 will likely be family-oriented and/or service oriented. People with a 6 Birth Force are in their element when being kind, caring, supportive, and responsible. People on this path will be devoted to nurturing, protecting, and serving others, especially those closest to them. This is also the number of the healer, so the 6 Birth Force may be drawn to the healing arts, healthcare field, or social service work.

Birth Force Number 7: The path of the 7 Birth Force involves developing one's intellectual and analytical skills to gain knowledge, wisdom, and understanding. Those who follow this path often develop expertise in their fields, and some go on to teach. This is also a spiritual number associated with the metaphysical, mystical, and psychic.

Birth Force Number 8: The path of the 8 Birth Force involves ambition, drive, and achievement. This path often leads people to strive for authority, power, wealth, and success. Common occupations for people on this path include banker, attorney, judge, director, or CEO/CFO of organizations in business, finance, or government.

Birth Force Number 9: The path of the 9 Birth Force involves serving humanity. People on this path are intuitive, broadminded, and accepting of others. They understand that we are all connected, so they tend to be sympathetic. The universality of love and showing tolerance and compassion towards others is important to them. Their service to others may take the form of philanthropy or charitable work, the arts, religion, politics, education, health, or other humanitarian efforts.

Birth Force Number 11: The path of the 11 Birth Force involves being an inspirational leader and spiritual messenger. People with an 11 Birth Force are meant to serve humanity, whether as spiritual teachers, humanitarians, peacemakers, negotiators, or in some other capacity in which they are in the public eye. People on this path are seekers, often drawn to the mystical. They tend to be intuitive, prophetic, visionary, and psychic. They are quite charismatic leaders who can be very powerful and influential.

Birth Force Number 22: The path of the 22 Birth Force involves being a master organizer, planner, and builder for humankind.

Birth Force Number 33: The path of the 33 Birth Force involves serving humanity as a master teacher of unconditional love, healing, and enlightenment.

Destiny Number

The Destiny Number represents where you are heading in this incarnation, in other words, the course of events of your life. I add the Impression Number (total of all the letters of the name) and the Birth Force Number (birthdate) to get the Destiny Number.

If the Birth Force Number represents the *what* regarding your life's mission, the Destiny Number represents the *where*. It takes more than just your name to get you where you are going. The Destiny Number represents the people, places, and things that will cross your path along the journey and assist you in learning your lessons.

To find your Destiny Number, write your Impression and Birth Force Numbers in the spaces below, add them, and reduce to a single digit. Be mindful of any Master Numbers you find when adding and reducing.

_____	+	_____	=	_____
Impression Number		**Birth Force Number**		**Destiny Number**

Now that you have found your Destiny Number, you can refer to the list of meanings below to get a sense of where you may be heading in this incarnation.

Destiny Number 1: You are destined to be a leader. Remember that 1 is the number of the Creator and of beginnings. It will be important for you to use your creativity and originality to give birth to new ideas and to have the courage to put them into action. Have confidence in yourself to stand on your own and be self-sufficient. Take the initiative to pursue your goals. Your determination will pay off in the long run.

Destiny Number 2: You are destined to be a peacemaker. Whether you are a loving, supportive spouse or partner in your relationship, a partner in business, or a diplomat, you are meant to bring balance, peace, and harmony to your relationships through understanding and cooperation.

Destiny Number 3: You are destined to express yourself. You may become an artist, musician, writer, comedian, actor/actress, or entertainer. Or you may just be the socialite who is the life of the party. Regardless, you are meant to share your talents.

Destiny Number 4: You are destined to be industrious and hard working. Your love of organization, rules, and efficiency will make you a natural manager or builder. Your hard work will pay off as you lay a solid foundation on which to build a stable, secure life and lasting legacy.

Destiny Number 5: You are destined for adventure and change. Your love of freedom may lead you to seek work that involves travel and meeting new people. Your willingness to be unconventional and take risks will make you progressive and keeps things changeable and exciting.

Destiny Number 6: You are destined to raise a family and/or to do service work. You may find yourself in the role of caretaker. This is also the number of the healer.

Destiny Number 7: You are destined to be studious, analytical, and intellectual. You may be drawn to philosophy, metaphysics, or spirituality. You are meant to teach the knowledge you have gained, even if not formally.

Destiny Number 8: You are destined for achievement and success. Whether in business or government, you are meant to supervise, direct, or lead others. This is the number of executives, attorneys, and bankers.

Destiny Number 9: You are destined to be a humanitarian. You may serve mankind through charitable and philanthropic endeavors or by being an inspiration to others in some way.

Destiny Number 11: You are destined to be a spiritual messenger. This could take the form of an idealistic or visionary leader, a peacemaker or negotiator, a mystic or psychic, a prophet or seeker. You may find yourself becoming a spiritual teacher or a famous inspirational speaker. Regardless, you are meant to influence many people in matters of a spiritual nature.

Destiny Number 22: You are destined to be a master organizer, planner, and builder. You are meant to make the idealistic practical for the benefit of many.

Destiny Number 33: You are destined to help humanity as a guide and teacher. You may become a reformer, a human rights activist, or a leader of a movement. You are meant to help people with their healing.

Chapter 6

Putting It All Together

Example: John Fitzgerald Kennedy

As a reminder, begin by adding all the vowels of the name together and reducing to get the Soul Number. The Soul Number is the past life. Then add all the consonants of the name together and reduce to get the Identity Number. Add the Soul Number and Identity Number together (adding all the letters of the birth name together and reducing) to get the Impression Number. Then, add the date of birth and reduce to get the Birth Force Number.

Finally, add the Impression Number (sum of birth name) and Birth Force Number (sum of birth date) to get the Destiny Number.

Let's refer to the chart and consider John Fitzgerald Kennedy as an example.

1	2	3	4	5	6	7	8	9
A	B	C	D	E	F	G	H	I
J	K	L	M	N	O	P	Q	R
S	T	U	V	W	X	Y	Z	

First, write out the name. Find the number that corresponds with each letter in the name. Put the numbers associated with the vowels (A, E, I, O, U, and Y) above the name. Put the numbers associated with the consonants below the names. This makes it easier when you add across to get the Soul Number (all the vowels added together) and the Identity Number (all the consonants added together).

```
6                        9   5 1                    5   5 7
John                     Fitzgerald                 Kennedy
1 85                     6 287 9 34                 2  55 4
```

Now, add the vowels across the top: 6+9+5+1+5+5+7 = 38 (3+8) = 11 (1+1) = 2.

Since the number 11 is a Master Number, his Soul Number would be written 11/2. I usually add and reduce above each name, as this provides me with information about the physical (first name), mental/emotional/professional (middle name), and spiritual (last name) aspects of the person in his/her past life. So, how I add the vowels above each name would look like the example below.

$= 6$	$9+5+1 = 15/6$	$5+5+7 = 17/8$
6	9 5 1	5 5 7
John	Fitzgerald	Kennedy

However, in this example, when I add and reduce the vowels in each name and then add them all together to get the Soul Number ($6+6+8 = 20/2$), I miss the Master Number. Most of the time it doesn't matter whether you add them all the way across and reduce or add and reduce above each name and then add the values of the vowels for each of the names and reduce. You usually will get the same number regardless. However, you may want to add them both ways just to make sure you aren't missing any Master or Karmic Numbers.

Now, do the same for the consonants across the bottom to get his Identity Number.

John	Fitzgerald	Kennedy
1 85	6 287 9 34	2 55 4
$1+8+5 = 14$	$6+2+8+7+9+3+4 = 39$	$2+5+5+4 = 16$

Now, reduce the 14 ($1+4$) = 5
Reduce the 39 ($3+9$) = 12 ($1+2$) = 3
Reduce the 16 ($1+6$) = 7

Add the $5 + 3 + 7 = 15$ ($1+5$) = 6. John Fitzgerald Kennedy's Identity Number is a 6.

From this point on, you will see me write a number and reduce it in an abbreviated and more efficient format. To use the examples above, I would write the 14 as 14/5, the 39 as 39/12/3, and the 16 as 16/7. So, I would figure John Fitzgerald Kennedy's Identity Number as follows:

14/5 + 39/12/3 + 16/7 = 5+3+7 = 15/6 (Identity Number)

Now that you have his Soul Number (11/2) and Identity Number (15/6), you can add them to determine his Impression Number.

11/2 (Soul Number)
+ 15/6 (Identity Number)

26/8 (Impression Number)

Find the Birth Force Number by adding together the month, day, and year of the birth date. John Fitzgerald Kennedy's date of birth is 5-29-1917 = 5 + 29/11 + 18/9 = 5 + 11 + 9 = 25/7 (Birth Force Number).

The last of the key numbers is the Destiny Number. Determine the Destiny Number by adding the Impression Number to the Birth Force Number. JFK's Impression Number (8) + Birth Force Number (7) = Destiny Number (15/6).

Now, create an Inclusion List to determine what numbers are present and absent in his name. Remember that several numbers missing in a name suggests a young soul, and the numbers that are missing are indicative of what karmic lessons he came here to learn. If there are no numbers missing in the name, the person is an old soul.

An overabundance (4 or more) of any one number in the name suggests an imbalance in that area.

To create JFK's Inclusion List, make a list numbering 1 – 9 (see below). Then, look for how many letters in his name equal 1 (A, J, S). John Fitzgerald Kennedy has 2 letters in his name that equal 1, the J in John and the A in Fitzgerald. Next, look for how many letters in his name equal 2 (B, K, T). He has two letters in his name that equal 2, the T in Fitzgerald, and the K in Kennedy. Now, determine how many letters in his name equal 3, 4, 5, and so on until you've finished all 9. See the finished list for John Fitzgerald Kennedy below.

1 = 2 (J, A)
2 = 2 (T, K)
3 = 1 (L)
4 = 2 (D, D)
5 = 6 (N, E, E, N, N, E)
6 = 2 (O, F)
7 = 2 (G, Y)
8 = 2 (H, Z)
9 = 2 (I, R)

JFK had every number represented in his name, suggesting that he was an old soul. With the exception of the number 5, his numbers were well balanced (he has one or two of each number). When we discussed the meanings of the Inclusion Numbers in Chapter 4, we learned that an overabundance of 5s suggests a person who tends to spread himself too thin.

Review

Here's a quick review of how we calculate each of the key numbers.

Soul Number: total of the number values of all the vowels in the name.

Identity Number: total of the number values of all the consonants in the name.

Impression Number: Soul Number (vowels) + Identity Number (consonants).

Birth Force Number: Birth Month + Birth Day + Birth Year

Destiny Number: Birth Force Number (birth date) + Impression Number (birth name)

Chapter 7

Past, Present, and Future

Phases of Life, Pinnacles, and Challenges

In numerology, time is cyclical, with each cycle lasting nine years and then repeating. However, when we are considering the person's entire lifetime, we divide it into four phases, like the four seasons (spring, summer, autumn, and winter). The first phase is the longest.

To determine the length of the first phase, subtract the Birth Force Number from 36. The 36 is derived from 360° in a full circle. Subsequent phases each span the nine-year numerology cycle.

Each phase has Pinnacles (representing potential achievements or attainments) and Challenges (representing potential difficulties to overcome). There are Birth Force Pinnacles and Challenges and Personal Year Pinnacles and Challenges. We will consider Personal Year Pinnacles and Challenges in the next chapter.

Before we calculate someone's Birth Force Pinnacles and Challenges, we need to determine at what ages each of the four phases will occur.

Let's look at an example of a woman whose birthday is 12-15-1964, and whose Birth Force Number is 11/2. To determine what constitutes the first phase of her life, we subtract her Birth Force Number (11/2) from 36 (36 − 2 = 34 years). She will be in the first phase (spring) of her life from birth to 34 years old.

Since it takes 9 years to complete each subsequent cycle, she will be in phase 2 (summer) of her life from 34 to 43 years old (34 + 9 = 43). She will be in phase 3 (autumn) from 43 to 52 years of age (43 + 9 = 52). Phase 4 (winter) begins at 52 years old and lasts until her death.

We don't stop growing once we get to phase 4. We continue our 9-year cycles, and each year presents its own Pinnacles and Challenges. For now, let's focus on how to determine your Birth Force Pinnacles and Challenges. I will teach you how to find your Personal Year Pinnacles and Challenges in the next chapter.

Birth Force Pinnacles

The Pinnacles represent our potential achievements or attainments. However, these are not just handed to us. We have to earn them by living up to the positive qualities of the number of that Pinnacle while learning the lessons associated with our Birth Force Challenge number for that phase of our life at the same time. To calculate the Birth Force Pinnacle, start from the date of birth and add going up. Continuing with the example above, see the next diagram.

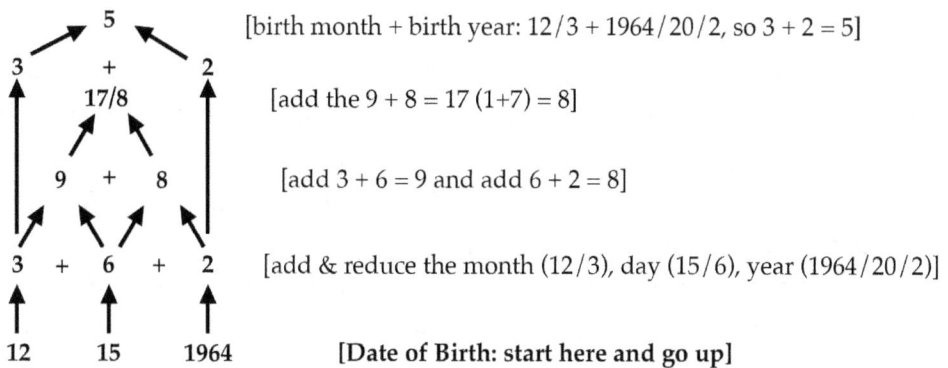

5   [birth month + birth year: 12/3 + 1964/20/2, so 3 + 2 = 5]

3   +   2   17/8   [add the 9 + 8 = 17 (1+7) = 8]

9   +   8   [add 3 + 6 = 9 and add 6 + 2 = 8]

3   +   6   +   2   [add & reduce the month (12/3), day (15/6), year (1964/20/2)]

12   15   1964   **[Date of Birth: start here and go up]**

There is a Pinnacle associated with each of the four phases of a person's life. So, there will be four Pinnacles. Now that you know how to do the basic calculations, I'll show you which numbers represent the Pinnacles for each phase of life by circling them on the diagram below.

How to identify the Birth Force Pinnacles for the 4 phases of life:

In Phase 1, during the spring of her life (from birth to 34 years old), this woman's Pinnacle Number is 9 (humanitarian, completions). In Phase 2, during the summer of her life (from 34 to 43 years old), her Pinnacle Number is 8 (achievement, success, money). In Phase 3, during the autumn of her life (from 43 to 52 years old), her Pinnacle Number is an 8 again. In Phase 4, the winter of her life (from 52 years old until death), her Pinnacle Number is 5 (change). For additional information about the characteristics of these numbers, you can always refer to the number meanings charts in Chapter 3.

Birth Force Challenges

The Birth Force Challenges represent the potential difficulties you will encounter during the four phases of your life. These challenges come from within you rather than outside of you. In other words, these challenges represent your weaknesses, deficiencies, or shortcomings. As a result, the Birth Force Challenges represent major lessons you've come here to learn, and they are different from your karmic lessons. The Birth Force Challenges require mastery of the self in order to achieve your Pinnacles.

To calculate the Birth Force Challenges, start from the date of birth and subtract going down. Drop any negative signs. We don't use negative numbers. See the example below:

12   15   1964   **[Date of Birth: start here and go down]**

3 - 6 - 20/2   [add & reduce the month (12/3), day (15/6), year (1964/20/2)]

    3 - 4   [subtract 3 - 6 = -3 (drop negative sign) and subtract 6 - 2 = 4]

    1   [subtract 3 - 4 = 1]

3 - 2   [birth month - birth year: 12/3 - 1964/20/2, so 3 - 2 = 1]

    1

Similar to the Pinnacles, there are Challenges associated with each of the four phases of a person's life. So, there will be four Challenges.

Now that you know how to do the basic calculations, I'll show you which numbers represent the Challenges for each phase of life by circling them on the diagram below, using this same example.

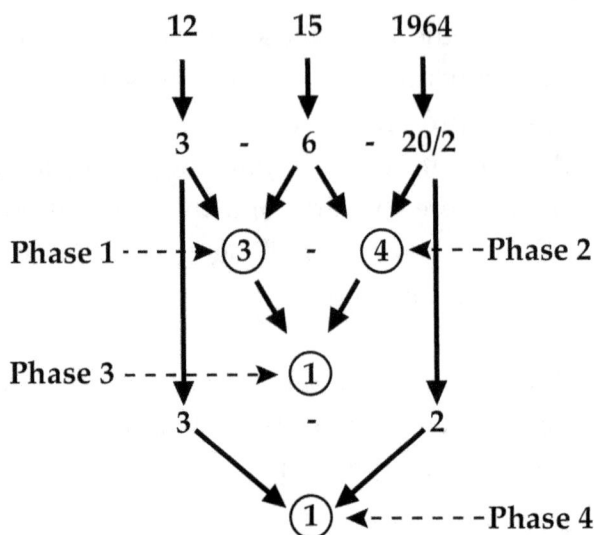

In Phase 1 (birth to 34 years old), this woman's Challenge Number is 3 (creativity, self-expression). In Phase 2 (34 to 43 years, her Challenge Number is 4 (hard work, organization, industry). In Phase 3 (from 43 to 52 years old), her Challenge Number is a 1 (leadership, beginnings, maintaining independence, self-sufficiency, finishing projects). In Phase 4 (from 52 years old until death), her Challenge Number is 1 again. For the general meaning of other numbers, refer to the number charts in Chapter 3.

It is worth mentioning that you can have zero for a challenge number. You can't get zero on a Pinnacle, because you are adding numbers. Zero symbolizes the world. With zero there is no ending or beginning. When you have a zero challenge, you have freedom of choice. So, don't allow anyone else to guide you during this time. You need to say what is best for you. When I see zeros in the challenges, that tells me it is going to be a very challenging period. Many zeros in the challenges are dramatic and represent one lesson after another.

Now that you know how to determine the Birth Force Pinnacles and Challenges for the four phases of a person's life, you can use the same method for determining Personal Year Pinnacles and Challenges by substituting the current calendar year for the year of birth. I'll show you how to do this in the next chapter.

Chapter 8

Personal Years, Months, and Days

Personal Year

Knowing your Personal Year Number can be incredibly helpful. Since you now know the characteristics of the numbers, you can probably guess what you could expect from a 1 Personal Year. A 1 Personal Year would be a time of new beginnings. A 9 Personal Year, on the other hand, would be a time of endings and completions. If you wanted to start a business, starting it when you are in a 1 Personal Year would be an excellent time to do so, but not when you are in a 9 Personal Year. Don't start anything in a 9 Personal Year that you want to last for more than about 18 months. This is true of relationships as well.

The Personal Year calculation is as follows:

Birth Month + Birth Day + Current Calendar Year = Personal Year

Let's consider what your Personal Year would be if you were born on April 19th. If the current calendar year is 2018, your Personal Year would be 4 + 19/10/1 + 2018/11/2 = 4 + 1 + 2 = 7. You would be in a 7 Personal Year in 2018.

The Personal Year goes from birthday to birthday and starts about three months before our birth, because we were in the womb. You will start feeling the vibration of the number of the next Personal Year about three months before your birthday. So, if your birthday is April 19th, you would start feeling the effects of the 7 Personal Year beginning in late January of 2018.

What if your birthday occurs later in the year? Let's say your birthday is December 15th. If the current calendar year is 2018, your Personal Year would be 12/3 + 15/6 + 2018/11/2 = 3 + 6 + 2 = 11/2. You would be in a 2 Personal Year, but not until December of 2018. For most of 2018, you would be in a 1 Personal Year (12/3 + 15/6 + 2017/10/1 = 3 + 6 + 1 = 10/1). This often confuses people, but remember, the Personal Year goes from birthday to birthday, not calendar year to calendar year.

If your birthday is on December 15th, you won't start feeling the effects of the 2 Personal Year until around mid-September 2018.

So, if you were born later in the year (October, November, or December), I wouldn't change your Personal Year until it gets closer to your birthday.

Take a moment now to determine what your current Personal Year is using the formula below.

Birth Month	+	Birth Day	+	Current CalendarYear	=	Personal Year

See below for information about what you can generally expect in different Personal Years:

1 Personal Year: A 1 Personal Year is a time of new beginnings. It starts a new cycle for you. This would be a good year to take the initiative in some new endeavor, whether that is starting a business, applying for a new job, or putting some new idea into action. It's a time to be independent, self-sufficient, and self-determined. It is also a good time to take a leadership role or to be a pioneer in some way.

2 Personal Year: A 2 Personal Year is a time of partnerships and relationships. Rather than taking a leadership role, as in the 1 Personal Year, a 2 year is a time to be in a supportive role. It is a time for you to nurture your relationships and partnerships by being patient, calm, diplomatic, and tactful with others. This is a time to be the peacemaker and to strive for balance and harmony.

3 Personal Year: A 3 Personal Year is a time to be social, creative, and self-expressive. Whether you are writing, lecturing, painting, acting, playing music, or exercising your creativity in some other way, it is important to allow your imagination and inspiration to flow. If the 3 stems from a 12/3, you'll feel the need to be a free-spirit and say, "Don't fence me in." If, on the other hand, the 3 stems from a 21/3, you'll likely feel restricted, as if your hands are tied.

4 Personal Year: A 4 Personal Year is generally a time of practicality, organization, and hard work. However, if the 4 stems from a 13/4 (Karmic Number), it's a different story. I refer to a 13/4 Personal Year as a suicidal year, but I do not mean that you or anyone else is going to commit suicide. What I'm saying is a 13/4 Personal Year is dramatic. It indicates change of friendships, relationships, your home, your job, and/or your money. Everything starts to happen, forcing us to do things that we kept thinking we were going to do but never did. It forces us to recognize we've got to make a change.

5 Personal Year: A 5 Personal Year is generally a time of change. It can be a time of adventure, risk taking, or travel. However, if the 5 comes from a 14/5 (Karmic Number), you will need to be careful of chemical imbalances or pleasure seeking, self-indulgences that can be harmful to yourself or others. A 23/5 is a number I associate with education. So, a 23/5 Personal Year will be a time for you to pursue knowledge and learning. Seek to educate yourself in some way to further yourself personally, professionally, or spiritually.

6 Personal Year: A 6 Personal Year is generally a time to be mindful of your responsibilities, particularly around family matters. A 24/6 is the number I associate with the Sacred Heart, meaning you will be working from the heart. A 24/6 Personal Year can bring heartache or relationship problems. A 15/6 Personal Year would be a time for healing, as 15/6 is the number of detachment and the healing aspects of life.

7 Personal Year: A 7 Personal Year is usually a time of introspection. You may feel the need to turn inward and concentrate on yourself. You may feel reclusive and be somewhat of a hermit. It is a time for study, meditation, and spiritual pursuits. A 16/7 (Karmic

Number) Personal Year can present challenges. If 16/7 is one of your key numbers, then this would be a year for you to pay off some karma. Remember that 16/7 warns of losses in this lifetime. These may manifest as tragedies, disgrace, loss of power or fortune, or deception in relationships. It involves a cycle of destruction and rebuilding of your life. Satisfying this debt requires learning the spiritual truths involving willpower and what is right. If you are in a 16/7 Personal Year, be careful to do the right thing, particularly in your love relationships.

8 Personal Year: An 8 Personal Year is a time of business, property, money and/or professional matters. If a 17/8, it can mean government, business, or education. It is a time for you to reap the benefits of what you started in the 1 Personal Year. An 8 Personal Year can be a time of achievement and success provided that you stay focused and are efficient, organized, goal-directed, and action-oriented. This is a time for you to be wise, level-headed, and business-like in your decisions and actions. If you do, it will pay off nicely. An 8 Personal Year is also a year of karma. When a person is in an 8 Personal Year, they normally are paying off a lot of karma.

9 Personal Year: A 9 Personal Year is a time of completions and endings. It is a time to wrap up loose ends and to get rid of stuff you don't need anymore. Since it is a time of endings, you never want to start anything in a 9 Personal Year that you want to keep for more than 18 months. Don't sign any contracts in a 9 Personal Year. There is increased risk of complications. The 9 Personal Year is also a time to be a humanitarian, serving your fellow human beings in some way, and practicing compassion, forgiveness, acceptance, and tolerance of others.

Personal Year Pinnacles and Challenges

In Chapter 7, you learned that there are Birth Force Pinnacles and Challenges for the four phases of a person's life. Similarly, when we determine the Personal Year Pinnacles and Challenges, we divide each year (12 months) into four quarters, with three months to every quarter. Each Personal Year will present Pinnacles and Challenges for each quarter of the year. Your Pinnacles and Challenges will change every year when your Personal Year changes. That is what makes a chart readable every year.

To determine your Personal Year Pinnacles, first find your Personal Year using the birth month, birth day, and current calendar year. I'll use the woman with the December 15th birthday that I used to show you how to calculate the Birth Force Pinnacles and Challenges, so you can see what is different when calculating the Personal Year Pinnacles and Challenges.

If her birth month is December (12), her birth day is the 15th, and the current calendar year is 2018, you would calculate her current Personal Year as follows:

Personal Year = Birth Month + Birth Day + Current Calendar Year

Personal Year = 12+15+2018
(1+2) + (1+5) + (2+0+1+8)
3+6+11/2
3+6+2 = 11/2 Personal Year

Now, let's determine what her Pinnacles and Challenges will be for 2018. The Personal Year Pinnacles and Challenges are calculated in much the same way as the Birth Force Pinnacles and Challenges with one exception. Instead of using the year of birth, you use the current calendar year. Like the Birth Force Pinnacles, the Personal Year Pinnacles are calculated by starting at the bottom with the birth month, birth day, and calendar year and adding as you go up.

The Personal Year Challenges, on the other hand, are calculated by starting at the top and subtracting as you go down, just like you did with the Birth Force Challenges.

I know this can be confusing, so let's look at our previous example of the December 15th birthday and the current calendar year (2018) to determine what the Personal Year Pinnacles and Challenges are.

Pinnacles for 2018 (birth month December = 12/3; birth day 15th = 15/6; calendar year 2018 = 11/2):

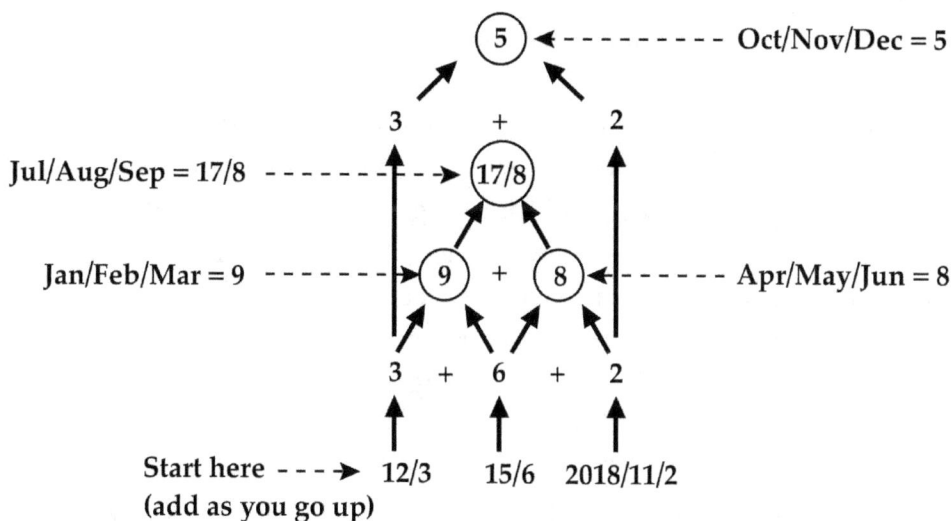

Let me explain exactly what I did. I started by adding the birth month (12/3) to the birth day (15/6), and 3+6 = 9. So, in the first quarter (3 months) after the December birthday, the Pinnacle number is 9.

The second step involves adding the birth day (15/6) to the current calendar year (2018/11/2), and 6+2 = 8. So, in the second quarter (April, May, and June), the Pinnacle number is 8.

The third step involves adding those two Pinnacle numbers together (9+8 = 17/8). So, in the third quarter (July, August, and September), the Pinnacle number is 8 again.

In the final step, I add the birth month (12/3) to the current calendar year (2018/11/2), and 3+2 = 5. So, in the final quarter (October, November, December), the Pinnacle number is 5.

Now, what does all this mean? Well, if you think of Pinnacles as our potential achievements or attainments, it means that she (with the December 15th birthday) will have opportunities to realize the positive effects of the 9 (completions, compassion, acceptance, tolerance, forgiveness, etc.) from January through March if she is able to overcome her Personal Year Challenges (which we will determine shortly) during that time. If you consider that she is in an 11/2 Personal Year (partnerships and relationships), the first three months after her birthday will present opportunities for her to be compassionate, accepting and forgiving in her relationships.

April through September will present opportunities to realize the positive effects of the 8 Pinnacles (success, achievement, money), and October through December will present opportunities to realize the positive effects of the 5 Pinnacle (change, travel, adventure) if she can overcome her Personal Year Challenges during those times.

Now, let's determine what her challenges will be, so she will know what she needs to master in order to be successful in 2018. Remember, with the challenges, you start at the top with the birth month, birth day, and calendar year and subtract as you go down.

Challenges for 2018 (birth month December = 12/3; birth day 15th = 15/6; calendar year 2018 = 11/2):

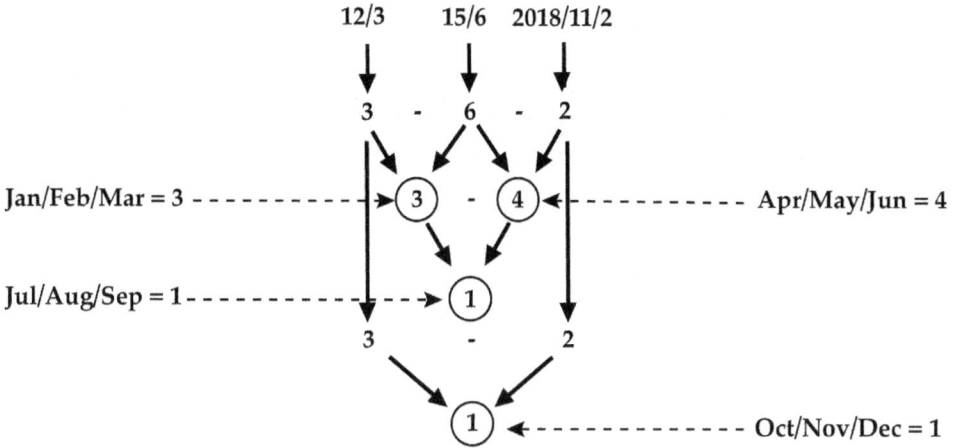

```
                    12/3      15/6    2018/11/2
                     |         |         |
                     ↓         ↓         ↓
                     3    -    6    -    2

Jan/Feb/Mar = 3 --------------→ (3) - (4) ←---------- Apr/May/Jun = 4

Jul/Aug/Sep = 1 -----------------→ (1)
                     3         -         2

                              (1) ←------------- Oct/Nov/Dec = 1
```

The calculations for the Personal Year Challenges are usually a little easier to understand, but I'll explain them anyway, just so there isn't any confusion. The first thing I do is subtract the birth day (15/6) from the birth month (12/3), and 3-6 is -3, but I drop the negative sign. So, her Personal Year Challenge for the first three months after her December 15th birthday (January, February, March) is a 3 (creativity, self-expression).

The second step involves subtracting the calendar year (2018/11/2) from the birth day (15/6), and 6-2 = 4. Her Personal Year Challenge for April, May, and June is a 4 (hard work, organization, laying a foundation).

To determine the Personal Year Challenge for July, August, and September, subtract the second quarter Challenge (4) from the first quarter Challenge (3), and 3 − 4 = -1. Drop the negative sign. So, the third quarter Challenge is a 1 (taking initiative, maintaining independence, self-sufficiency, and finishing projects).

Find the Challenge for the final quarter (October, November, and December) by subtracting the current calendar year (2018/11/2) from the birth month (12/3). In this case, 3 − 2 = 1. So, the Challenge for the final quarter is a 1 again.

With these examples, you should now be able to determine your own Personal Year Pinnacles and Challenges. Refer to Chapter 3 for the characteristics of these numbers to get a sense of what may be in store for you.

Personal Month

Now that you know your Personal Year, you can determine your Personal Month by adding it to the current calendar month:

Personal Month = Personal Year + Current Calendar Month

Remember, to find your Personal Year, you add your birth month, birth day, and current calendar year. So, if your birth day is August 4th, and the current calendar year is 2018, your Personal Year would be 8+4+2018/11/2 = 14/5. You would be in a 5 Personal Year. If the current calendar month is January, you would add your Personal Year (5) + current calendar month (January = 1), and 5+1 = 6. So, your current Personal Month would be a 6.

Take a moment now to determine what your current Personal Month is using the formula below:

_____		_____		_____
Personal Year	+	Current Calendar Month	=	Personal Month

The characteristics of each Personal Month can be found below:

1 Personal Month: A time to take initiative, be independent, and self-sufficient

2 Personal Month: A time to seek balance, harmony, and peace

3 Personal Month: A time for socializing, entertaining, creativity, and self-expression

4 Personal Month: A time to be practical, industrious, and hardworking

5 Personal Month: A time of change, excitement, adventure seeking

6 Personal Month: A time for healing, responsibilities, family, and service work

7 Personal Month: A time of introspection, analysis, study, and spirituality

8 Personal Month: A time of power, achievement, mastery, business, and money

9 Personal Month: A time of completions, being charitable, selfless, and a humanitarian

11 Personal Month: A time of being visionary, idealistic, inspirational, and influential

Personal Day

Knowing your Personal Year also allows you to determine your Personal Day by adding it to the current calendar month and day:

Personal Day = Personal Year + Current Calendar Month + Current Calendar Day

So, if you are in a 3 Personal Year, and today's date is July 3rd, your Personal Day would be calculated as follows: $3 + 7 + 3 = 13/4$. You would be in a 4 Personal Day.

Take a moment now to determine what your current Personal Day is using the formula below:

_____   _____   _____   _____

Personal Year   +   Current Calendar Month   +   Current Calendar Day   =   Personal Day

The characteristics of each Personal Day can be found below:

1 Personal Day: Be confident, start something new. Promote yourself and your ideas.

2 Personal Day: Be diplomatic, cooperative, and understanding. Pay attention to details.

3 Personal Day: Be spontaneous and playful. Express yourself in creative ways. Entertain and be social.

4 Personal Day: Be disciplined. Take time to organize, so you are being efficient and methodical. Be conscientious and work hard.

5 Personal Day: Be unconventional today. Be versatile, travel, take a risk, and be open to new experiences.

6 Personal Day: Devote yourself to your responsibilities at home or in your community today. Be loving, caring, kind, open-minded, tolerant, and unselfish. Serve others.

7 Personal Day: Find some quiet, alone time to think, study, meditate, or pray today.

8 Personal Day: This is a money-making day. It is a good day to invest, do business dealings, etc. Be ambitious, but exercise self-control and good judgment.

9 Personal Day: Be compassionate toward others today; practice coming from a place of acceptance and tolerance. Choose to be forgiving, broad-minded and philanthropic.

11 Personal Day: Follow your intuition, be an inspiration to others, seek spiritual enlightenment. Today is a good day to be in the limelight.

22 Personal Day: Be courageous, confident, and masterful in realizing your visions for helpings others. Find a practical and productive way to benefit mankind.

33 Personal Day: Be of service to others by modeling unconditional love.

Now that you know how to find your Personal Year, Personal Month, and Personal Day, you can use this information to your advantage. If you have something serious coming up, such as a surgery, signing a contract, buying a house, or making some other major purchase or decision, take a few minutes to determine your Personal Day, Month, and Year. You can find out what this month is all about for you. Find out what your Personal Day is, pick the most opportune day, and then go for it. Knowing this information can tell you whether you are really going in the right direction this month. For example, I wouldn't want to have surgery on a 9 Personal Day.

Chapter 9

How to Set-Up and Read a Numerology Chart

As I mentioned before, my system is not a defined system, because a number may have a different meaning depending on where it is in your chart, and I let Spirit decide. When I read for a person, even when I've read for them before, I still do their chart again, because the chart is going to tell a different story each time. While it may seem that the chart isn't going to change, you've grown and changed. The letters will make the change. Having a birthday will make a change. Spirit directs me when I do a reading, so – even when I have done a chart before – I will see something new.

Regardless, I like to have at least 6-months pass before I read for someone again.

After you have determined your five key numbers, your Inclusion List, your Birth Force Pinnacles and Challenges, and your current Personal Year, it is time to set up your numerology chart.

Begin by putting your first name on the top row, your middle name on the second row, and your last name on the third row. Your first name is the physical name. It represents your physical self. Your middle name is your mental, emotional, and professional name, and it represents these aspects of yourself. Your last name is your spirit name, and it represents your spiritual self.

To illustrate, I'm going to set up a chart for President Barack Obama on the next page. To begin, I need his full name at the time of his birth (Barack Hussein Obama), and I need his date of birth to determine what Personal Year he was in when he was born. Did you assume that we are born into a 1 Personal Year, since 1 represents new beginnings? Well, it doesn't quite work that way. If you recall, you determine the Personal Year by adding the birth month, birth day, and the current calendar year.

Barack Obama was born August 4, 1961. His Personal Year at the time of his birth was 8+4+1+9+6+1 = 29/11/2. By the way, you also just determined his Birth Force Number (11/2). I believe like the monks believe, that you are practically one year old when you are born. For the sake of simplicity, I will start the chart at the time he turned 1 y/o (he was in a 3 Personal Year) and go to age 13. See if you can guess why I have written out his name this way. Do you see the patterns?

Year	'62	'63	'64	'65	'66	'67	'68	'69	'70	'71	'72	'73	'74
Age	1	2	3	4	5	6	7	8	9	10	11	12	13
Physical (1st Name)	B	B	A	R	R	R	R	R	R	R	R	R	A
M/E/P (2nd Name)	H	H	H	H	H	H	H	H	U	U	U	S	S
Spiritual (Last Name)	O	O	O	O	O	O	B	B	A	M	M	M	M
Essence	16/7	16/7	15/6	23/5	23/5	23/5	19/10/1	19/10/1	13/4	16/7	16/7	14/5	6
Personal Year	3	4	5	6	7	8	9	1	2	3	4	5	6

Although I stopped at age 13, hopefully I provided enough information for you to see how I set up a chart. Let's just look at his first name. Notice how there are two B's? If you remember the number values for each letter, B has a value of 2. So, it takes two years to get through the B in Barack. The letter A has a value of 1, so it takes one year to get through the A in Barack. However, R has a value of 9, so it will take 9 years to get through the R in Barack. At 13 years old, he is in the second letter A on his physical name.

If I had extended the chart out for 5 additional years, you would see that he would complete the name Barack at age 18. It would take him one year to complete the A at 13 years old, then three more years to complete the C (14 – 16 years old), and then two more years to complete the K (17 – 18 years old).

I do the same thing with the middle name (on the row beneath the first name) and with the last name (on the row beneath the middle name), as I did with the first name. I write them out in the same fashion.

There is significance to completing a name. When you complete your physical name, you review yourself and consider what changes you would like to make physically. When you complete the cycle of your name on the Mental/Emotional/Professional, it generally means a change of jobs or occupation. If this occurs in a 23/5 Personal Year, it would be an indication that you can't go any further in your profession until you get additional education, because 23/5 represents education. When you complete your name on the spiritual, you may review where you are spiritually, and Spirit will review your progress as well. Overall, completing a cycle of the name indicates new awareness, and that is why it is significant.

When I teach numerology classes, this is the point at which a student will ask, "What do you do when you have multiple middle names?" Some numerologists drop them or add them all together. I wouldn't drop any of them. I think they play a very important role. I look at the first of the middle names to find out where someone is mentally. The second middle name tells me where someone is emotionally. I combine the two to determine what the person may do professionally. If someone has 3 middle names, I would use all 3 middle names, separating them into mental, emotional, and professional respectively. See below for examples of how I would separate out the names in a chart.

Person with four names:
First name: Physical
Second name: Mental
Third name: Emotional
Fourth name: Spiritual

Remember, in the case above, I would combine the second (Mental) and third (Emotional) names to determine the professional aspects of this person.

Person with five names:
First name: Physical
Second name: Mental
Third name: Emotional
Fourth name: Professional (profession also includes schooling)
Fifth name: Spiritual

If someone says they do not have a middle name, I tell them, "Well, you're going to get a new name today. Were you ever given a confirmation name?" And if so, I'll use it. But I'll also ask Spirit to step in sometimes, and I'll tell them, "Before this reading is over, you are going to get a middle name." Now, officially they don't need to go out and register it. The reason I believe it is so important for people to have a middle name is that people without middle names will have more difficulty dealing mentally and emotionally with life's lessons. There is nothing there in the way of resources to help them learn. So, they can be just all physical or spiritual.

Some people only have a letter as their middle name, and I've done a chart with that if they insisted. However, I still ask them what the reason was for that letter. A lot of times people have said things like, "Well, I really just didn't want to use my middle name, because I was named after my daddy. That's why I don't even claim it." I'll tell them, "You've got to learn to claim it, because you are rejecting your mental and your emotional aspects." Not claiming your middle name causes you to be scattered.

Another question I've been asked is, "What if I use a nickname?" I have used that sometimes just to see in what part of their life they use that nickname. However, I still use the full name given at the time of birth to construct the chart.

Hopefully, what I have done so far in terms of setting up the chart for Barack Obama during his first 13 years of life makes sense. There is still one part of the chart we have yet to discuss – the Essence.

The Essence is calculated by adding the number values of each of the letters of the first, middle, and last names present during that year. For example, during Barack's first two years of life, the letter on his physical name was a *B*. On his mental/emotional/professional name it was an *H*. On his spiritual name, it was an *O*. When you add the values of these letters, B (2) + H (8) + O (6) = 16/7. So, I would say that he was in a 16/7 Essence during his first two years of life.

In order to fully understand the significance of Barack's Essence Numbers, it is imperative that we know his key numbers. When our Essence Number matches one of our key numbers, it is an especially significant time for us. In what way depends upon which of our key numbers the Essence Number is matching, since our key numbers represent different things about us. Let's take a minute to determine his five key numbers:

Barack Obama was born August 4, 1961.

1+1 = 2	3+5+9 = 17/8	6+1+1 = 8	2+8+8 = 18/9 (Soul Number)
1 1	3 59	6 1 1	
B a r a c k	H u s s e i n	O b a m a	
2 9 3 2	8 11 5	2 4	
2+9+3+2 = 16/7	8+1+1+5 = 15/6	2+4 = 6	7+6+6 = 19/10/1 (Identity Number)

Soul Number (vowels) = (1+1 = 2) + (3+5+9 = 17/8) + (6+1+1 = 8) = 2+8+8 = 18/9

Identity Number (consonants) = (2+9+3+2 = 16/7) + (8+1+1+5 = 15/6) + (2+4 = 6) = 7+6+6 = 19/10/1

Impression Number = Soul Number (vowels) + Identity Number (consonants)= 9+1 = 10/1

Birth Force Number (Month, Day, and Year of Birth) = 8+4+1+9+6+1 = 29/11/2

Destiny Number = Birth Force Number (11/2) + Impression Number (10/1) = 11+10 = 21/3 (some numerologists might write his Destiny Number as 11,10 since 11 is a Master Number and 10 is a Karmic Number, rather than reducing and adding them). I do think it is important to note these significant numbers. As I have mentioned before, I write the Master Numbers and still reduce them, because I have no way of knowing whether or not someone is truly living up to his/her potential. Given that Barack Obama was elected to a second term as President of the United States of America, however, it might be safe for me to assume that he was living up to his potential, at least in some regards. Like I mentioned previously, Spirit directs me.

We can see from his chart that he was in a 3 Personal Year (self-expression) at 1 year old and a 4 Personal Year (organizing, being industrious) at 2 years of age. So, during his first year of life, he was finding his voice and expressing himself by crying, cooing, or babbling. At two years of age, he was likely trying to understand and make sense of his world (organizing), and he was busy exploring and getting into everything (the terrible twos). Anyone could guess that. You don't need a numerology chart to tell you that information. That is going to be true for almost any infant or two-year-old child. The Essence Number, however, tells you even more. We see that he was in a 16/7 Essence. You may recall that the number 16 is one of the Karmic Numbers. So, that should tell you that the first two years of his life were significant and likely difficult. The 16/7 suggests that he may have experienced a loss at that time that required rebuilding of his life in some way.

Since I don't know anything about President Obama's early years, I did a search on Wikipedia to see if I could find some information that might help me to understand what I was seeing in his chart. According to Wikipedia:

"Obama was born on August 4, 1961, at Kapiʻolani Maternity & Gynecological Hospital (now Kapiʻolani Medical Center for Women and Children) in Honolulu, Hawaii,[2][4][5] and is the first President to have been born in Hawaii.[6] His mother, Stanley Ann Dunham, was born in Wichita, Kansas, and was of mostly English ancestry.[7] His father, Barack Obama, Sr., was a Luo from Nyang'oma Kogelo, Kenya. Obama's parents met in 1960 in a Russian class at the University of Hawaiʻi at Mānoa, where his father was a foreign student on scholarship.[8][9] The couple married in Wailuku on Maui on February 2, 1961,[10][11] and separated when Obama's mother moved with her newborn son to Seattle, Washington, in late August 1961, to attend the University of Washington for one year. In the meantime, Obama, Sr. completed his undergraduate economics degree in Hawaii in June 1962, then left to attend graduate school at Harvard University on a scholarship. Obama's parents divorced in March 1964.[12] Obama Sr. returned to Kenya in 1964 where he remarried; he visited Barack in Hawaii only once, in 1971.[13] He died in an automobile accident in 1982.[14]

In 1963, Dunham met Lolo Soetoro, an Indonesian East–West Center graduate student in geography at the University of Hawaii, and the couple were married on Molokai on March 15, 1965.[15] After two one-year extensions of his J-1 visa, Lolo returned to Indonesia in 1966, followed sixteen months later by his wife and stepson in 1967, with the family initially living in a Menteng Dalam neighborhood in the Tebet subdistrict of south Jakarta, then from 1970 in a wealthier neighborhood in the Menteng subdistrict of central Jakarta.[16] From ages six to ten, Obama attended local Indonesian-language schools: St. Francis of Assisi Catholic School for two years and Besuki Public School for one and a half years, supplemented by English-language Calvert School homeschooling by his mother.[17]" See http://en.wikipedia.org/wiki/Barack_Obama#Early_life_and_career for more information.

From this information, it appears that Barack was going through some major changes during the first several years of his life. Remember that he was in a 16/7 Essence (loss and rebuilding of his life) from ages 1 – 3. According to Wikipedia, his mother separated him from his father and moved him from Hawaii to Seattle as a newborn, and they stayed there for a year while she went to school. Then, after a year, his mother moved him back to Hawaii. Then, in 1963 (Barack was 2 years old), she got involved with someone new. This certainly seems like loss and rebuilding of his life to me.

At three years of age (1964), Barack's Essence Number changed to a 15/6. I associate the number 15/6 with detachment and the healing aspects of life. Barack was also in a 5 Personal Year (change) at that time. That year, Barack's mother divorced his father, and his father returned to Kenya and remarried. In March 1965, his mother remarried. Barack was still 3 years old and in a 15/6 Essence (detachment/healing) and a 5 Personal Year (change) at that time, because his birthday wasn't until August. Remember, numerology years go from birthday to birthday, not calendar year to calendar year.

Come August of 1965, when Barack turned 4 years old, his Essence changed to a 23/5 (education and change), and he was in a 6 Personal

Year (family and responsibilities). I don't know if he went to pre-school or if his mother and stepfather educated him at home, but learning became important to him at that time.

In 1966, his stepfather returned to Indonesia. Again, I don't know the exact date, but Barack turned 5 years old and was in a 23/5 (education and change) Essence. His stepfather moving to Indonesia presented more change for him. However, Barack was in a 7 Personal Year (introspection, study, being a hermit). So, he may have been more withdrawn into himself during that time.

According to Wikipedia, Barack and his mother separated from his stepfather for 16 months before they moved to Indonesia to join him in 1967. Barack was 6 years old and still in a 23/5 Essence, but his Personal Year changed to an 8. An 8 Personal Year is a time of achievement and education for children.

Wikipedia says that Barack attended local Indonesian-language schools from ages 6 to 10, spending two years at a Catholic school followed by a year-and-a-half at a public school. Ages 7 and 8 were significant for him. I believe that we start working on our life lessons at 7 years old, and this certainly seemed to be the case for Barack.

Barack's Essence changed to a 19/10/1 at age 7, and his Identity Number is a 19/10/1 (Karmic Number), so he was questioning his identity. He had moved from Hawaii to a different country (Indonesia) and was attending schools where people spoke a different language. He was trying to figure out, "Who am I? What am I? Where do I belong?"

Having his Essence Number (19/10/1) match his Identity Number also indicates he was working through karma from 7 – 9 years old. You may recall that hell = 8+5+3+3 = 19/10/1. So, this was likely a very difficult time for him. He was trying to adjust to all of these changes, struggling with his identity, and probably felt like he was going through hell.

When 19/10/1 is the Essence Number, it involves rising from the lower self into the higher self. The lesson associated with the 19/10/1 when it is one of the key numbers is the proper use of power. Barack would have been challenged to become independent and stand up for himself without dominating others and being aggressive.

Since identity was so important to him during that time, he may have thought about what he wanted to be when he grew up and imagined himself as a great leader one day (the 1 Identity Number is the number of the leader).

This would not be surprising if you take into consideration his other key numbers. His Soul Number is a 9, suggesting that he is bringing the humanitarian in from his past life. His Impression Number is the positive Karmic Number 10/1, or what I refer to as the God Force number. With 1 representing the leader and 0 representing the world, the 0 actually amplifies the power of the leader. In addition, Barack's Birth Force Number is an 11. You may recall that the path of the 11 Birth Force involves being an inspirational leader and spiritual messenger. People with an 11 Birth Force are meant to serve humanity, whether as spiritual teachers, humanitarians, peacemakers, negotiators, or in some other capacity in which they are in the public eye. They are quite charismatic leaders who can be very powerful and influential.

However, Barack was only 7 years old at the time. So, let's consider what else may have been happening in his life then. In addition to being in a 19/10/1 Essence, he was also in a 9 Personal Year. Remember, a 9 Personal Year is a time of completions and endings. If he only attended the Catholic school for two years (ages 6 and 7), that fits with his chart, since he was in a 9 Personal Year at age 7. According to Wikipedia, he then changed schools the next year. This also coincides with him being in a 1 Personal Year (a time of new beginnings) at 8 years old. He was still in a 19/10/1 Essence, however, so this was still a difficult time for him.

His chart suggests the next few years were difficult for Barack as well. In 1970, when Barack turned 9 years old, his Essence Number changed to a 13/4. I call this the suicidal year. I'm not saying that he felt suicidal. I call it the suicidal year because it involves a change of friendships, relationships, job/school, and home.

According to Wikipedia, in 1970, the family moved from Menteng Dalam neighborhood in the Tebet subdistrict of south Jakarta to a wealthier neighborhood in the Menteng subdistrict of central Jakarta. Barack was in a 2 Personal Year, a time of partnerships and relationships.

In 1971, at age 10, Barack was in a 16/7 Essence again, like his first two years of life, and he was in the 16/7 Essence for two years. Remember, 16 is a Karmic Number, and a 16/7 Essence suggests that he likely experienced another loss that required rebuilding of his life yet again.

Quoting Wikipedia: "In 1971, Obama returned to Honolulu to live with his maternal grandparents, Madelyn and Stanley Dunham, and with the aid of a scholarship attended Punahou School, a private college preparatory school, from fifth grade until his graduation from high school in 1979.[19] Obama lived with his mother and sister in Hawaii for three years from 1972 to 1975 while his mother was a graduate student in anthropology at the University of Hawaii.[20] Obama chose to stay in Hawaii with his grandparents for high school at Punahou when his mother and sister returned to Indonesia in 1975 to begin anthropology field work.[21] His mother spent most of the next two decades in Indonesia, divorcing Lolo in 1980 and earning a PhD in 1992, before dying in 1995 in Hawaii following treatment for ovarian cancer and uterine cancer.[22]"

The 16/7 Essence suggesting a loss that required rebuilding of his life is confirmed by the information in Wikipedia, indicating that he moved from Indonesia back to Hawaii to live with his grandparents in 1971, and then in 1972 moved again, this time moving in with his mother and sister. He spent two years (ages 10 – 11) dealing with loss and rebuilding of his life. At 10 years old he is in a 3 Personal Year (a time to be social, creative, and self-expressive). At 11 years old he is in a 4 Personal Year (a time to work hard and lay a solid foundation). In 1973, when Barack turns 12 years old, his Essence changes to the Karmic 14/5 and his Personal Year changes to a 5 (change). Remember, the 14/5 is associated with the lesson of moderation and not going to extremes. We have no way of knowing what Barack was going through at that time.

I don't plan to do a complete chart of President Obama's life in this book, but I do want to emphasize that you could pick up where I left off and continue his chart to the current calendar year and beyond. I just wanted to illustrate how to set up a numerology chart and begin to interpret it.

To reiterate, the numerology chart provides useful information for understanding what people may have been experiencing at particular times in their lives. In addition – and of particular interest to those coming to me for a reading – the chart allows me to project into their future to get an idea of what they can expect in upcoming years.

When I do a reading, I don't make a numerology chart of the person's entire life. I determine how many years it takes to get through their physical name, how many years it takes to get through their mental/emotional name, and how many years it takes to get through their spirit name. Then, I figure out at what age they would have completed each name closest to the age they are now.

For example, if a 46-year-old woman came to me for a reading, and it would take 43 years for her to complete her physical name, I would start at the beginning of her name again at 44 years old. Once we complete a cycle of a name, it starts over again with the first letter of that name. I typically set up the chart 6 years before and 6 years after the person's current age. That gives me enough space to see what is really going on.

Now, all you need to be able to interpret someone's numerology chart is an understanding of what each Essence Number represents and the significance of certain letters in the chart. I'll devote the rest of this chapter to the meaning of the Essence Numbers. In the next chapter, I will cover the significance of certain letters in the chart.

Essence Numbers

1 Essence: new beginnings, time to take initiative, time to take a leadership role.

19/10/1 (Hell = 19/10/1) is a Karmic Essence Number that represents the lower self. It can indicate an identity crisis. It is a spiritual number suggesting the person is trying to raise from the lower self to the higher self at that time.

28/10/1 (Heaven = 28/10/1) is a Karmic Essence Number that represents the higher self. A 28/10/1 Essence is a time when the person is seeking truth, higher consciousness, and working on loving oneself.

2 Essence: partnerships, relationships, time to be in a supportive role.

2 over 2 (2 Essence in a 2 Personal Year) is the bankruptcy sign, but if you warn people to be careful with their money during that time, they may be able to prevent it.

20/2 is a spiritual number. I call it the nun or monk sign.

29/11/2 is a Master Essence Number meaning the person is working in the light, becoming enlightened, or being spiritually protected. An 11/2 Essence tells me the person is trying to grow spiritually at that time.

3 Essence: a time to be social, creative (artwork, music, acting, writing, etc.), and a time of self-expression.

12/3 is a time to be a free spirit, but it can also be a time when a person is scattered and letting their emotions control them.

21/3 is a time when a person feels restricted, like their hands are tied. They may perceive that others are trying to control them. They are not doing what they want in the way that they want.

4 Essence: a time to organize, work hard, pay attention to details, and lay a solid foundation for life.

13/4 is a Karmic Essence Number that indicates a very hard year. The 13/4 is what I call the suicidal number. That doesn't mean the person is going to commit suicide. It means the change of friendships, relationships, home, job, sometimes finances, etc. You say, "My God, what else is going to happen to me?" When I see a double 13/4 – meaning the Essence is 13/4 and they are in a 13/4 Personal Year – that tells me their life is dramatic that year. If you were born in a 13/4, there was probably some difficulty at the time of your birth. You may not have wanted to be born, or your mother may have had some issues, or you might have had issues at the time of your birth. The 13/4 can also mean putting down new roots.

5 Essence: a time of change, travel, and adventure.

14/5 is a Karmic Essence Number that can suggest a misuse of personal freedom. This can manifest as sexual transgressions, addictions, or chemical imbalances in the body. The person may be experiencing this personally or crossing paths with someone who has an addiction or chemical imbalance. It can also suggest someone who is spending too much time in his or her work. If 14/5 is their Soul Number, it can mean their soul is awakening at the time it shows up in their chart as their Essence Number.

23/5 is a time in which the person is pursuing education.

6 Essence: a time of responsibilities, especially around family matters.

15/6 is a time of detachment, letting go, and healing.

7 Essence: a time of introspection, study, meditation, spiritual pursuits, and concentrating on the self.

16/7 is a Karmic Essence Number that can suggest a time of loss that requires rebuilding of one's life in some way.

8 Essence: A time of achievement, money, and business. A double 8 (8 Essence in an 8 Personal Year) can mean government, property, and/or business matters. Eight is also a year to pay off karma. When an 8 Essence occurs in a 4 Personal Year, it can mean changing foundation, property, and/or homes.

9 Essence: A time of completions, of wrapping up projects and tying up loose ends. A time to declutter and purge the unnecessary. When a person is in a 9 over 9 (9 Essence in a 9 Personal Year), they will experience significant life changes. Their life turns a total flip-flop, and they won't be the same after this year. There will be a lot of completions and endings, and people will say they are not the same person they used to know.

Now that you know the general meaning of the Essence Numbers and Personal Year Numbers, you will have a pretty good idea of what you can expect in any given year. However, this time period will be especially significant for you if the Essence Number is the same as one of your five key numbers.

For example, when I see your Soul Number someplace in the chart, it tells me that something from a past life was really bothering you at that time, and you were trying to deal with it. That would prompt me to look at your Inclusion List to see what letters you are missing, since those represent your karmic lessons. I would also consider your Personal Year Number.

Let me give you an example. As I am looking at a woman's chart, I see that her current Essence Number is the same as her Soul Number. I see from her Inclusion List that she is missing the number 6. And, she is in a 6 Personal Year. Six is a karmic number for her because it is the only number she is missing. Six represents family, so she is dealing with some family issues at that time. Quite often, this is a time of healing. What is missing – in her case the 6 – is what she really needs to work on this year. When the Essence Number is the same as your Soul Number, it can mean your soul is awakening at that time.

Similarly, if the Essence Number is the same as your Identity Number, this will be a time in which you are working on your identity (how you see yourself and what you came into this lifetime thinking you were going to do professionally, spiritually, etc.). You will be considering the choices you are making in this lifetime.

If the Essence Number is the same as your Impression Number, this time period will be significant in terms of how others view you.

When the Essence Number matches your Birth Force Number, it will be a time for you to truly come into your own, as the Birth Force

Number represents your path in this life, or what your higher self wants to accomplish in this lifetime.

By now you can probably guess what it means when your Essence Number is the same as your Destiny Number. This would be a time in which the course of events of your life would be very important. Your environment, the people surrounding you, the places you go, and the things that happen to you during this time will all assist you in learning your life lessons.

Chapter 10

Letters of Significance in a Numerology Chart

The letters that have special significance in the numerology chart include the following: A, C, E, H, I, J, L, N, O, R, S, T, U, Y. Although I will do my best to explain what each letter represents, to fully understand the significance of the letter, you have to pay attention to where it is in the chart. The letters will mean different things depending on what name they are in on the numerology chart. If the letter is in the first name, it will involve the person's physical aspects. If the letter is in the middle name, it will involve their mental/emotional/professional aspects. Finally, if the letter is in the last name, it will involve their spiritual aspects.

The body of the name creates that letter. Also, be sure to consider the Essence and Personal Year Numbers occurring concurrently with that letter to get the full picture of what is going on in the person's life at that time.

When reading someone's chart, the first letters I look for are the letters *A*, *J*, and *S*. They represent changes. Each of those letters has a value of 1, so they will only appear in the chart once (for one year) in the cycle of the name before the name transitions to the next letter.

When you see an *A*, *J*, or *S*, circle it to call your attention to the fact that the person will be experiencing big changes in that area. Of course, as I mentioned above, what kinds of changes the person will be making depends on whether or not the *A*, *J*, or *S* is on the physical name, the mental/emotional/professional name, or the spiritual name.

An *A* really jumps out at me. It tells me a story. An *A* can be very emotional and dramatic, so it is likely to be an emotional year. The *A* tells me to pay attention. After circling the *A*, I would look to see if there is a 24/6 on the whole last name. A 24/6 can mean a past life situation where the person finally paid off karma.

Next, I'd look to see if the *A* is something mental or emotional. If the *A* is in the mental name, it suggests a cognitive shift, such as a new awareness, perspective, or understanding.

The letter *S* is usually a big move when it occurs in the physical name. The *A* or *S* on your mental/emotional/professional name represents changes, detachment, and letting go.

In addition to noticing what name the *A*, *J*, or *S* is in, remember to look at the Essence and Personal Year Numbers that appear in the chart at that time to determine what types of changes the person will be experiencing.

As I discussed in the previous chapter, if the Essence Number is the same as one of the key numbers, it will have special significance. Take a look at the chart below.

The woman whose chart is shown here has an Identity Number of 17/8 and a Soul Number of 19/10/1. When you look at the chart, you can see that she will be in a 17/8 Essence at 49 years old. Similarly, the chart shows that she will be in a 19/10/1 Essence at 52 years old. This information alone would suggest that ages 49 and 52 are going to be very significant years for her and will present opportunities to pay off some karma.

Her chart also shows she will experience changes in more than one area of her life from 49 – 51 years old. When I see the three 1's (any combination of *A-J-S*) consecutively, it tells me the person will be experiencing a transformation at that time. It will feel like an emotional death and rebirth to her. See if you can determine in what areas she will be experiencing transformation before reading my interpretation below.

Age	49	50	51	52
Physical (First Name)	(S)	E	E	E
Mental/Emotional/ Professional (Second Name)	I	(A)	(S)	Y
Spiritual (Last Name)	G	G	G	G
Essence	17/8	13/4	13/4	19/10/1
Personal Year	8	9	1	2

If you said the person will be experiencing major physical changes when she is 49 years old, followed by major changes mentally/emotionally/professionally over the next two years, then you would be right. If I was reading for this person, here is what I would tell her:

"You are going to experience a transformation over the next few years, but the transformation is going to be requiring more than one thing. At 49, you are going to make a big move. There's a lot of change there. It's got to do with property and business because of the 8s. Your Essence Number and Personal Year are both 8s, and 8 is the number associated with business and property. At 49 the 8 on top of 8 occurs with an S. The S signifies a change. So, the S with an 8 Essence in an 8 Personal Year represents changes in business and property. The S is on your physical name, so there could be a move, a lot of physical changes, and because of the business signs, it could mean the sale of property. You may be moving your business or having a lot of business transactions that change your business. The S on your physical name shows you are going to be physically involved in all of it.

I also see the letter I here on your Mental/Emotional/Professional name at this time. The letter I represents emotions. So, this is going to be a very emotional year for you. You need to prepare your emotions for all the changes and new things that are happening. This also makes sense when we consider that your Identity Number is a 17/8, and you are in a 17/8 Essence in an 8 Personal Year. So, this will be a very dramatic year for you. That part of you, your identity, is so important this year, becoming who you are. You are finding your identity.

So, at 49 it's changes in business and property, physical move, emotional, and, you've got three 1s in a row at 49, 50, and 51. The 1s come from the S on your physical name at 49, the A on your mental/emotional/professional name at 50, and the *S* on your mental/emotional/professional name at 51. Those three 1s in a row are what tell me you will be going through a transformation. Once it starts, it's going to be like dominoes. You are starting something physically at 49 that's going to create something that you can do mentally/emotionally/professionally. I don't see you doing what you're doing right now as your true profession. I see you being creative and working out karma and bringing things forward. The letter *E* also represents change. The *E* has a value of 5, and the number 5 is associated with changes. You have an *E* on your physical name at ages 50, 51, and 52. This suggests that you will be experiencing physical changes during this time.

Mentally, emotionally, and professionally you are going to be making a big change at 50. You will be in a 9 Personal Year, and that is a time of endings and completions, and you're in a 13/4 Essence. The 13/4 indicates a very hard year. It can mean the death of friendships, relationships, your home, your job, and sometimes your finances. It can also mean putting down new roots, which will likely be the case for you at 51 when you're in a 1 Personal Year. So, there's a lot of closure between 50 and 51. You will have to make a move and get rid of a business in order to start a new business at 51 when you will be in a 1 Personal Year, and that is a time of new beginnings.

Then, you are going to be paying off a lot of karma starting at 52. Your Soul Number is 19/10/1, and you will be in a 19/10/1 Essence at 52. That's when your soul becomes awakened so much that nothing will stop you. You have finally taken a step forward and let some things go behind you, and you really are concentrating on the true beauty of you."

I hope this example gives you an idea of how I would integrate all of the information I have taught you so far in interpreting the numerology chart when giving someone a reading. Although our previous example using Barack Obama's information in Chapter 9 was still informative, as you now know, it was not complete, because it did not include the meaning of the letters in his chart.

Before I proceed with the meanings of each letter, I want to share a few additional rules I follow to help me interpret the chart. When I do a reading, I normally do your chart 6 years before your current calendar year birthday and 6 years after. It's not practical to do someone's entire life chart for a reading. Besides, they usually aren't coming to me to hear about their childhood. They want help dealing with what is going on in their lives right now, and what they can expect in upcoming years.

I've already told you that I circle the letters *A*, *J*, and *S*, because they tell me that something dramatic is going on in their life. I got that in a dream. I also put a square at the end of a name (the last letter that completes each name in the chart). Completing a name indicates new awareness at that time. When a person completes the last name (spirit name), Spirit will review where he or she is spiritually.

There are a few other letters I want you to flag when you see them in the chart. The first letter is *O*. The letter *O* has a value of 6, so it will appear in the chart for six years before the next letter in the name appears in the chart. Put a slash (/) in between the third and fourth *O* and pay attention to what is going on in the person's life at that time. Remember that *O*, value of 6, usually involves responsibilities, marriage, family issues. *O* is also the letter associated with spiritual protection.

The next letter is *P*, value of 7, so a name with a *P* in it will list the *P* seven times in the chart. Find the *P* in the middle (the fourth *P*) and circle it. Then, look at what is going on in the chart at that time. The person will be balancing what *P* represents (usually something involving secrecy of some sort when in the physical or mental/emotional/professional name. When the *P* is in the spirit name, it indicates a time of gaining spiritual wisdom).

The final letter I want you to flag is the *Y*. Like the *P*, *Y* has a value of 7. Find the *Y* in the middle (the fourth *Y*) and circle it. Then, look to see what is going on in the person's life at that time. This can be a time in which the person is at a crossroads and needs to make a decision about something. See letter *Y* below for more information.

The remainder of this chapter will be devoted to the general meanings for each of the letters of significance. To accurately interpret the chart, remember the rules I mentioned above. Also consider the key numbers, the Essence Number, the Personal Year, and the name in which the letter falls when you are analyzing the chart.

And, one last thing…when there's a double letter, it's twice compounded. In other words, when you are looking at a particular year in the numerology chart, if two of the letters are the same (meaning that the letter on the physical name and/or mental/emotional/professional and/or spiritual names is the same), then the effects of that letter will be double for the person that year. Also, when you see triple emotional letters, it tells you that will be a very difficult time emotionally for the person. The emotions may feel so overwhelming that it may even feel like a death to him or her. In the next chapter, I'll provide examples of how to integrate all this information when interpreting a numerology chart.

Letter Meanings

A: Change, new beginnings. This involves a change that can be very emotional and dramatic. If the *A* is in the physical name, it could be a physical change (depending on what other letters and numbers are with it), or it could mean they are getting ready to move. When *A* is on the mental/emotional/professional name, it represents changes, detachment, and letting go, and that is when the person is most likely to change jobs or professions. Remember, *A* has a value of one, so it will only last for one year.

C: happiness, social, caring

E: Changes, new activities. When *E* is on the physical name, it means experiences are coming about. When *E* is on the emotional name, it means the person is going through some changes and doesn't have control over his or her emotions. On the mental/emotional/professional name, it can mean that the person is ready to end an occupation and change jobs.

H: Education, hospitals, universities, schools, institutes, etc. On the physical name, the *H* may be related to health. On the mental/emotional/professional name, it is most likely related to education. On the spiritual name, *H* can indicate a test of one's resolve or a change of spiritual ways and direction.

I: a very emotional time

J: changes, new beginnings. Same as the letter *A* above.

L: Travel, sometimes over water. Situations causing moves or trips. Extensive in and out situations where you feel like you are being pulled back and forth. The letter *L* can be emotional, and like water or waves, things are up and down. When I see an *L* at the time of birth, it sometimes indicates an unusual birth, like a breach birth or having to be in the hospital for a little bit at the beginning. It could be that the person fought coming back, maybe knowing the responsibilities he or she agreed to, or something different, unusual, or unexpected that occurred at the time of birth.

N: Changes, new activities. On the physical name, *N* can mean physical changes. On the mental/emotional/professional name it can mean the person is not managing their emotions well at that time, or it can mean a job change. On the spiritual name, *N* can indicate new awareness.

O: Spiritual protection. Depending on where the *O* is in the chart, it can be an indication that Spirit is protecting the person. If it's on the physical name, it tells me that something happened at that time that made her start changing the way she wanted to live, who she wanted to live with, what she really wanted to do with her life. When *O* is in the physical name, it represents physical protection. On the mental/emotional/professional name, it means the person is being protected by Spirit at this time of life on the emotional level. When *O* is on the spiritual name, it represents a time of spiritual learning and understanding. Spiritually, the person is forging a new path and is being protected. Her spirit guides are walking ever so close. The letter *O* has a value of 6, so it will occur for 6 years in the numerology chart. Put a slash (/) in the middle between the third and fourth *O*. This is an indication of an emotional time. The letter *O* on the spiritual name can be a death sign, but NEVER tell the person you think they are going to die. Readings are supposed to be positive and helpful. So, you can't tell someone they are going to die, but you could say, "I see here there could be a death of the old you and a new birth." Especially if the person's Personal Year Number is the same as her Birth Force Number. When the Personal Year Number is the same as the Birth Force Number, it indicates a time of transformation. That doesn't necessarily mean a physical death. It may represent the death of the old self and rebirth of the new self.

R: R indicates a very emotional time. If the R occurs at the same time as the letter I, this year will be doubly difficult for the person, and they may feel overwhelmed.

S: Changes, new beginnings. When S is on the physical name, it usually means a big move. When S is on the mental/emotional/professional name, it represents a dramatic emotional change. If the S occurs with a 6 Essence Number or in a 6 Personal Year, it can involve family issues and mean separation, detachment, and learning to let go.

T: The letter T has a value of 2, so it will always appear twice in the chart. The double T in a chart represents partnerships and relationships. If they occur in the spiritual name at the beginning of a person's life, it suggests there may have been issues in his/her parents' relationship or marriage. In other words, there may have been family issues such as arguments or a struggle in trying to balance family situations. The double T represents the end of friendships, a relationship, detachment, and letting go. It can be very emotional.

U: money issues and the need to watch one's money

Y: In the physical name, *Y* can represent hormones, cancer, or leukemia. Since *Y* can be an indication of cancer, I'll ask if cancer runs in the family. For example, if I'm looking at a person's chart, and I see a *Y* when the person was 22-years old. I would ask, "At 22-years old, was there someone around you who had cancer?" If I see an *A* on the Spirit name in the chart at that time, that can mean a death. I would ask if someone around them died of cancer then. Now, if it occurs with a 13/4, it would tell me the person was going through a very hard time. Remember, 13/4 is a Karmic Number, and it indicates that the person is going through something difficult. So, I would ask if they or someone around them had cancer or a blood disorder then, because the chart tells me that the person either could have died or died. The *A* can also mean a death of the old self and a rebirth. It depends on where the *A* is in the chart, and on what is being added together.

Y can mean cancer, mentally or emotionally as well. To me, our thoughts and emotions can be cancerous. So, Spirit will tell me to question it, and you'll be surprised to find how often it is right.

A woman sometimes will have a double *Y* on top of each other and that represents hormone issues to me. Sometimes the *Y* on the mental/emotional/professional name can involve feeling the emotional effects of hormone changes going on in the body.

A double *Y* can suggest illness, and when the *Y* is circled, it can mean surgery. A double *Y* can also suggest issues with relationships. The letter *Y* on the mental/emotional/professional name can mean the person is very emotionally involved with someone he or she is caring for or watching over at this time. It could also indicate that the person will be working with people who have cancer, Leukemia, Aids, or blood disorders.

Chapter 11

Nuances of Interpreting a Numerology Chart

Rebirth

Rebirth is about what you have learned over a period of time. It is the time in which you come up for review. Rebirth requires that you face the reality of why you came here, and it drives you to become who you were meant to be. Rebirth doesn't start at the beginning of the cycle, like at a 1 Personal Year. For me, it has to do with your Birth Force Number. Rebirth will start on your birthday in the same Personal Year that is identical to your Birth Force Number. Beginning a few months before your birthday, you should start to feel something changing within you. You may find yourself asking, What's going on? What have I done with my life? What have I finished? Where am I in my life? You may feel some pressure to push onward for something and find yourself saying, I've really got to make some decisions here. I'm through with all this. I think of rebirth as a time to take inventory and ask, Am I the person I want to be? Am I the person I'm supposed to be? Am I going to accomplish some of the things I really want to do in my life? It is a time to recalibrate and get back on course, if necessary. It is also a time to consider what completions you are ready to make in your life now. This is not something I saw in another book. It is just something I realized when I saw that a person's Personal Year was identical to his or her Birth Force Number and asked myself, Why wouldn't that mean something more dramatic than just a regular Personal Year?

The Outer Names

In addition to the key numbers, Essence Numbers, Personal Year Numbers, and letters of significance, I look for what the numbers are on your outer names. By outer names I mean what the vowels add up to on each of your names individually, as well as what the consonants add up to on each of your names individually. The value of the vowels tells me about your past life on the physical (first name), mental/emotional/professional (middle name), and spiritual (last name). For example, if the vowels in your first name add up to an 8, you held power in a past life. You were someone of importance. I look to see if any of these numbers are the same as any of your five key numbers. If so, that tells me you brought this lesson forward from your past life. When any of these numbers are the same as the current Essence Number in the chart, it is an indication that you have an opportunity to work on this lesson and pay off some karma.

Similarly, I add the consonants of each name separately to get an idea of your identity on the physical (first name), mental/emotional/professional (middle name), and spiritual (last name). Then I look for any matches between any of these numbers and your five key numbers. I also look at the numerology chart for matches between any of these numbers and the current Essence Number, as that suggests a time when you are working on your identity in that area.

Let me give you an example. When adding the vowels (past life) of a woman's middle name, I notice that they add to a 17/8. When I'm looking at the consonants (identity), I notice that her identity on the middle name is also an 8. That tells me she brought the same lesson forward from her past life, but it's not as karmic, so she should be able to accomplish it in this lifetime. I've come to this conclusion because on the soul, the mental/emotional/professional (middle name) in the past life was a 17/8. This time the Identity Number on the middle name (mental/emotional/professional) is an 8. It is a straight 8, not a 17/8, so it is not as complicated, meaning that she should accomplish it in this lifetime. So, you want to pay attention to the outer names when they are identical to the Essence Number. That draws me immediately to what that year is about...for this woman, the year is about what she is doing mentally/emotionally/professionally this time.

Let's look at another example. I notice that the vowels in a man's middle name (mental/emotional/professional) add to a 13/4. That's past life. So, that tells me that his middle name is bringing most of his karma. However, I notice that the consonants (identity) in his first name (the physical) also add to 13/4. That tells me that he has physical issues (first name) as well as mental and emotional issues (middle name) from a past life karma. Looking at his chart to see when he is in a 13/4 Essence will be important, because he could be paying off some karma at that time.

Chapter 12

Procedure for a Numerology Reading

N ow that you've learned my system of numerology, you are
ready to put it into practice. The steps I take to do a
numerology reading are as follows:

1) Write out the person's full name at birth.
2) Write the number values of each vowel above the name.
3) Write the number values of each consonant below the name.
4) Add the number values of the vowels to get the Soul
Number.

5) Add the number values of the consonants to get the Identity Number.
6) Add the Soul Number and Identity Number to get the Impression Number.
7) Calculate the Birth Force Number by adding the month, the day, and the year of their birth.
8) Calculate their Personal Year by adding their birth month, birth day, and the current calendar year.
9) Determine their Personal Year Challenges (see Chapter 8) and tell them what their Challenges are going to be for that year. Remember to calculate their challenges for the current year by using their Personal Year, not their Birth Force Number. Using the Birth Force Number gives you their *life* challenges.
10) Write out their Inclusion List to see what numbers are missing from their name in order to determine what their karmic lessons are.
11) Set up their numerology chart (see Chapter 9) starting six years before to six years after their current age.

Note: In Chapter 9, I taught you how to set up Obama's chart beginning at age 1. To set up the chart starting six years before to six years after their current age, you need to determine how many years it takes to get through their first name (physical), middle name (mental/emotional/professional), and last name (spiritual).

Using the name Ann as an example, $A = 1$ (it takes 1 year to get through A), $N = 5$ (it takes 5 years to get through the first N and 5 more years to get through the second N). Add A (1) + N (5) + N (5) = 11 years to get through Ann. If Ann is 34 years old, she would have completed her name for the 3rd time at 33 and would be starting at A again at 34. So, I would put A on her physical name (top row) in the middle of the chart at 34 years old and put *Ns* for the 6 preceding years and *Ns* for the next 6 years. Then, I would use the same process for her middle and last names, until I have completed her chart from ages 28 (6 years prior to her current age) to 40 (6 years after her current age).

Below is an example of a chart for a 23-year-old male.

Age	17	18	19	20	21	22	23	24	25	26	27	28	29
Physical (1st Name)	R	R	R	R	R	T	T	N	N	N	N	N	E
M/E/P (2nd Name)	H	H	H	H	H	H	H	H	E	E	E	E	E
Spiritual (Last Name)	R	R	R	V	V	V	V	I	I	I	I	I	I
Essence	26/8	26/8	26/8	21/3	21/3	14/5	14/5	22/4	19/10/1	19/10/1	19/10/1	19/10/1	19/10/1
Personal Year	7	8	9	1	2	3	4	5	6	7	8	9	1

The first thing I look for on the chart are pattern changes in the letters. When the letters change, I draw a line between them to signify the change. For example, the letters change from RHR to RHV when he turns 20, so I would draw a line straight down between 19 years and 20 years old to show that change. The letters are the same (RHV) from ages 20 – 21 but change to THV at 22. So, I would draw another line straight down between 21 and 22 years of age to show that change. The letters are the same (THV) from 22 – 23, but they change to NHI at 24 years of age, so I would draw another line straight down between 23 and 24 years of age. He is only in NHI for one year before changing to NEI, so I would draw a line between 24 and 25 years of age. From 25 to 28, the letters stay the same (NEI), but then change again at 29 years old, so I would draw another line between 28 and 29 years old.

I take into consideration those changes in the context of his Essence Numbers (representing the issues he is dealing with at that time) and his Personal Year Numbers. I look for significant spiritual numbers. See below for an example of how his chart would look after I've drawn lines to identify his significant changes.

Age	17	18	19	20	21	22	23	24	25	26	27	28	29
Physical (1st Name)	R	R	R	R	R	T	T	N	N	N	N	N	E
M/E/P (2nd Name)	H	H	H	H	H	H	H	H	E	E	E	E	E
Spiritual (Last Name)	R	R	R	V	V	V	V	I	I	I	I	I	I
Essence	26/8	26/8	26/8	21/3	21/3	14/5	14/5	22/4	19/10/1	19/10/1	19/10/1	19/10/1	19/10/1
Personal Year	7	8	9	1	2	3	4	5	6	7	8	9	1

His five key numbers are as follows:

Soul Number (vowels in the name) = 7
Identity Number (consonants in the name) = 7
Impression Number (all the letters in the name) = 14/5
Birth Force Number (Date of Birth) = 7
Destiny Number (Birth Force + Impression Numbers) = 7 + 5 = 12/3

So, from ages 20 – 21, his Essence Number is a 21/3, and his Destiny Number is a 12/3. This suggests that he is going through a reversal. What I would tell him is from 20 – 21, physically, mentally/emotionally/professionally, and spiritually, he had to readjust that type of life.

In Chapter 10, you learned that *Ts* involve the end of friendships, a relationship, detachment, and letting go. It can be a very emotional time, and he is in the *Ts* from 22 – 23. His Essence Number during that time was the Karmic Number 14/5, which can be an indication of chemical imbalances, addictions, or spending too much time in his work.

The changes on the physical start when he turns 24 with the *Ns*. I see the 19/10/1's starting at age 25, so he will be challenged physically from 25 – 29. His letter on his mental/emotional/professional name during this time is an *E*, and on his spiritual name, his letter is an *I*. So, he's going to be affected. His personal life is going to change dramatically. There are going to be changes that may affect him emotionally (remember, the letters *I* and *R* represent emotional letters). Added together, it is 19/10/1. At 25 years old he starts that Essence. He may be finishing college at 24 years old where the *H* ends on his mental/emotional/professional name in the chart. The letter *H* is education, hospitals, universities, schools, institutes, etc.

When interpreting a numerology chart, I look at the totality of the Essence, taking into consideration what the Personal Year Number is and what letters are present on the physical, mental/emotional/professional, and spiritual names.

The final chapter of this book offers a complete numerology chart using former President Bill Clinton as an example. I will guide you through the entire process from beginning to end. Hopefully, that example will give you the confidence to do your own chart and the charts of your friends and family members. I always encourage my students to do charts of the people they know. The information will provide insight into the people closest to you, and the information they share with you can be confirmed by what you are seeing in the chart.

Chapter 13

A Complete Numerology Chart

President Bill Clinton

In this chapter, I will set up and interpret a numerology chart for President Bill Clinton. Bill was born August 19, 1946. His birth name was William Jefferson Blythe. According to Wikipedia (https://en.wikipedia.org/wiki/Bill_Clinton), his birth father died in an automobile accident a few months before Bill was born. In 1950, his mother re-married Roger Clinton Sr., and Bill formally adopted Clinton's surname when he turned 15 years old. I'll set up charts using his birth name and his adopted name, so we can compare the two.

First, identify the numbers associated with each letter, placing the numbers for the vowels above the name and placing the numbers for the consonants below the name.

```
9  91              5  5  6                 7  5
William            Jefferson               Blythe
5  33  4           1 66 91  5              2 3 28
```

Second, add and reduce the numbers of the vowels for each name and then add and reduce the total of the vowels to get the Soul Number. The name William contains the letter *I* twice (*I* = 9), and the letter *A* once (*A* = 1). Adding 9+9+1 gives us 19/10/1. Jefferson has two *Es* (*E* = 5) and one *O* (*O* = 6). Adding 5+5+6 gives us 16/7. Blythe has one *Y* (*Y* = 7) and one *E* (*E* = 5). When we add 7 + 5, we get 12/3. Now, to find William Jefferson Blythe's Soul Number, add the values of the vowels of each name together to get the total of the vowels and reduce.

William = 9+9+1 = 19/10/1
Jefferson = 5+5+6 = 16/7
Blythe = 7+5 = 12/3
Total of vowels = 1+7+3 = 11/2 (Soul Number)

Next add the consonants of each name and reduce to get his Identity Number.

William = 5+3+3+4 = 15/6
Jefferson = 1+6+6+9+1+5 = 28/10/1
Blythe = 2+3+2+8 = 15/6
Total of consonants = 6+1+6 = 13/4 (Identity Number)

Notice that the consonants of both William and Blythe total 15/6. This is an indication that the identity of William (on the physical) and Blythe (on the spiritual) are balanced. I will speak more about the significance of this below when we examine how his numbers change when his name changes to Clinton.

William Jefferson Blythe's Identity Number is a 13/4. Next, find the Impression Number by adding together the Soul Number and the Identity Number (which is the same as adding the values for all the letters of the name). William Jefferson Blythe's Soul Number = 11/2 and his Identity Number = 13/4.

11/2+13/4 = 24/6 (Impression Number)

Find the Birth Force Number by adding together the month, day, and year of the date of birth. William Jefferson Blythe was born on 8-19-1946 = 8 + 19 (1+9 = 10, reduce, 1+0 = 1) + 1+9+4+6 = 20 (2+0) = 2. So, add 8 + 1 + 2 = 11. His Birth Force Number is 11/2.

Now that we know his Impression Number (6) and his Birth Force Number (2), we can add the two to find his Destiny Number (6+2 = 8). So, his Destiny Number is 8.

Now, we will create his Inclusion List, by counting the number of letters with values from 1 to 9, as follows:

1 = 3 (*A* in William, *J* in Jefferson, and *S* in Jefferson)
2 = 2 (*B* in Blythe, *T* in Blythe)
3 = 3 (two *L*s in William, *L* in Blythe)
4 = 1 (*M* in William)
5 = 5 (*W* in William, two *E*s and one *N* in Jefferson, *E* in Blythe)
6 = 3 (two *F*s and one *O* in Jefferson)
7 = 1 (*Y* in Blythe)
8 = 1 (*H* in Blythe)
9 = 3 (two *I*s in William and one *R* in Jefferson)

His Inclusion List is not missing any numbers, suggesting that he is an old soul. The list is fairly well balanced, with the exception of an overabundance of the number 5. Fives represent change. Since we know his Birth Force Number, we can determine the length of each phase of his life. Remember, we always start with 36 and subtract the Birth Force Number to get the length of Phase 1. William Jefferson Blythe's Birth Force Number is 11/2, so 36 − 2 = 34. He will be in Phase 1 from birth to 34 years of age. Starting with 34, add 9 years for each cycle to get phases 2 through 4, as follows:

Phase 1 = 0 to 34 years old
Phase 2 = 34 to 43 years old (34+9 years = 43)
Phase 3 = 43 to 52 years old (43+9 years = 52)
Phase 4 = 52 years old to death

Now, let's determine what William Jefferson Blythe's Birth Force Pinnacles and Challenges will be for the 4 phases of his life. In previous examples, I calculated the Pinnacles and Challenges separately. In this example, I will put the two together, using the date of birth in the middle and adding as I go up for the Pinnacles while subtracting as I go down to determine the Challenges. The calculations are still the same.

To find the Pinnacles, add (and then reduce if necessary) the numbers going up (birth month + birth day = Phase 1, birth day + birth year = Phase 2, then add Phase 1 and Phase 2 together and reduce to get Phase 3. Phase 4 is calculated by adding the birth month to the birth year and reducing, if necessary, to get a single digit.

To find the Challenges, use the same numbers but subtract as you go down. See the example below for William Jefferson Blythe who was born on 8-19-1946:

Start with the birth date 8-19-1946 and reduce these to single digits. Eight does not need to be reduced, because it is already a single digit. However, 19 does need to be reduced, 1+9 = 10, but 10 still needs to be reduced, 1+0 = 1. So, 19 can be reduced to a 1. Using the shorthand method for writing this, it would be 19/10/1. Now, let's reduce the year 1946 (1+9+4+6 = 20, and 2+0 = 2). A shorthand method of writing this is 20/2. Now we can calculate the Pinnacles and Challenges. The example will incorporate the shorthand method to show you how to do it all together.

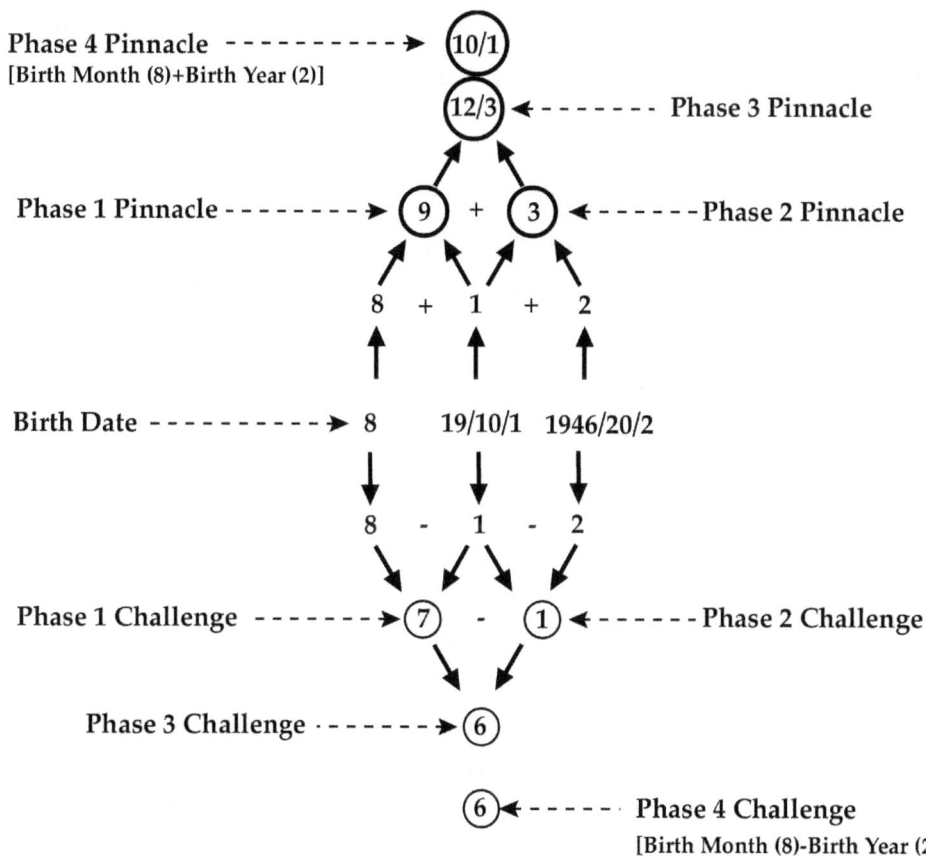

Phase 4 Pinnacle - - - - - - - - - → (10/1)
[Birth Month (8)+Birth Year (2)]

(12/3) ◄ - - - - - - - **Phase 3 Pinnacle**

Phase 1 Pinnacle - - - - - - - → (9) + (3) ◄ - - - - - - **Phase 2 Pinnacle**

8 + 1 + 2

Birth Date - - - - - - - - - → 8   19/10/1 1946/20/2

8 - 1 - 2

Phase 1 Challenge - - - - - - → (7) - (1) ◄ - - - - - - **Phase 2 Challenge**

Phase 3 Challenge · - - - - - - → (6)

(6) ◄ - - - - - · **Phase 4 Challenge**
[Birth Month (8)-Birth Year (2)]

Now, let's see how his numbers changed when his name changed from Blythe to Clinton.

9 91	5 5 6	9 6
W i l l i a m	J e f f e r s o n	C l i n t o n
5 33 4	1 66 91 5	33 52 5

Obviously, his names on the physical and mental/emotional/professional did not change. Only his last name (spiritual name) changed. Let's determine how his Soul Number changed by adding and reducing the values of the vowels for Clinton and adding that number to the values of the vowels for William and Jefferson.

To reiterate, the name William contains two *Is* ($I = 9$) and one *A* ($A = 1$). Adding 9+9+1 gives us 19/10/1. Jefferson has two *Es* ($E = 5$) and one *O* ($O = 6$). Adding 5+5+6 gives us 16/7. Clinton has one *I* ($I = 9$) and one *O* ($O = 6$), and $9 + 6 = 15/6$. Now, to find William Jefferson Clinton's Soul Number, add the values of the vowels of each name together to get the total of the vowels and reduce as follows:

William = 9+9+1 = 19/10/1
Jefferson = 5+5+6 = 16/7
Clinton = 9+6 = 15/6
Total of vowels = 1+7+6 = 14/5 (new Soul Number)

You may recall that the consonants in the name Blythe equaled 15/6. With the name change, now the vowels in the name Clinton equal 15/6. When Bill changed his spiritual name from Blythe to Clinton, the Blythe karmic debt got paid off, because it got pushed to the past (the vowels in Clinton became 15/6). The vowels represent our past lives. While the Blythe karmic debt was paid off, taking on the name of Clinton changed his Soul Number and caused him to take on new karmic lessons. See the Inclusion List below for William Jefferson Clinton:

1 = 3 (*A* in William, *J* and *S* in Jefferson)
2 = 1 (*T* in Clinton)
3 = 4 (two *L*s in William, *C* and *L* in Clinton)
4 = 1 (*M* in William)
5 = 6 (*W* in William, two *E*s and one *N* in Jefferson, two *N*s in Clinton)
6 = 4 (two *F*s and one *O* in Jefferson, *O* in Clinton)
7 = 0
8 = 0
9 = 4 (two *I*s in William, *R* in Jefferson, and *I* in Clinton)

With the name change, Bill is now missing 7s and 8s. The lack of 7s is an indication of karmic lessons requiring one to be introspective. The lack of 8s reflects lessons involving money, finances, and business.

We've determined that Bill's Soul Number Changed from 11/2 to 14/5 when his name changed from Blythe to Clinton. Now, let's determine how his Identity Number changed. Remember, the Identity Number is found by adding the total of the consonants of each name and reducing, if necessary, until you get a single digit.

9 91	5 5 6	9 6
William	**Jefferson**	**Clinton**
5 33 4	1 66 91 5	33 52 5

William = 5+3+3+4 = 15/6

Jefferson = 1+6+6+9+1+5 = 28/10/1
Clinton = 3+3+5+2+5 = 18/9
Total of consonants = 6+1+9 = 16/7 (new Identity Number)

Bill's Identity Number changed from a 13/4 to a 16/7 when his name changed to Clinton. Now, find his new Impression Number by adding together his Soul Number and his Identity Number.

New Soul Number = 14/5
New Identity Number = 16/7
Total = 14/5+16/7 = 30/3 or 12/3 (new Impression Number)

Bill's Impression Number changed from 24/6 to 30/3 when he changed names. The 30/3 is a high spiritual number, involving being challenged with morals and ideals. This is when his spirit was challenging him to be a free spirit.

Now that we know his new Impression Number and his Birth Force Number (which will never change), we can add the two to find his new Destiny Number.

Impression Number = 12/3
Birth Force Number = 11/2
Total = 12/3+11/2 = 23/5 (new Destiny Number)

Let's create a numerology chart for Bill from the ages of 52 to 69 years old. Remember, a chart takes into consideration how many years it takes to get through each name.

```
9  91            5  5   6              9   6
William          Jefferson             Clinton
5 33    4        1 66 91  5            33 52 5
```

William = 5 years to get through W+9 years to get through I+3 years to get through the first L+3 years to get through the second L+9 years to get through I+1 year to get through A+4 years to get through M = 34 years to get through William.

Jefferson = 1 year to get through J+5 years to get through E+6 years to get through the first F+6 years to get through the second F+5 years to get through E+9 years to get through R+1 year to get through S+6 years to get through O+5 years to get through N = 44 years to get through Jefferson.

Clinton = 3 years to get through C+3 years to get through L+9 years to get through I+5 years to get through N+2 years to get through T+6 years to get through O+5 years to get through N = 33 years to get through Clinton.

When I do a reading, I take the person's current age and create the chart going back 6 years and forward 6 years. If I was doing Bill's chart in 2010 and he was 64 years old at the time, I would determine what letter he was in on each of his names at that time. Since it takes 34 years to get through William (his physical name), he would complete it for the second time at age 68. I would start the chart for his physical name at 68 and work forwards and backwards from there, as follows on the next page.

Age	58	59	60	61	62	63	64	65	66	67	68	69	70
Physical (1st Name)	I	I	I	I	I	I	A	M	M	M	M	W	W
M/E/P (2nd Name)													
Spiritual (Last Name)													
Essence													
Personal Year													

Since the last *M* in William occurs at age 68, and I know that *M* has a value of 4 (in other words, it takes 4 years to get through *M*), I put an *M* in the 3 previous years. The letter before *M* in William is *A* (*A* = 1), so it only takes 1 year to get through the *A* in William. Because I'm still working backwards, I put one *A* in at age 64. The letter in William before *A* is *I* (*I* = 9). It takes 9 years to get through *I*, so I put the letter *I* in from the ages of 58 – 63. If I wanted to go back further than age 58, to where the letter *I* started for him, I would go back to age 55. So, now I have the Essence done for the physical name. Next, I need to determine what letter he is in on his Mental/Emotional/Professional Name (Jefferson).

It takes 44 years to get through Jefferson. So, he would have completed the final *N* at age 44. He would finish his second *F* at 62. *J* = 1 year + *E* = 5 years + *F* = 6 years + *F* = 6 years = 18 years. Since 44 + 18 = 62 years old, we will place the final *F* in Jefferson at 62 and work forwards and backwards from there. Remember, it takes 6 years to get through *F*, so he will have *Fs* from the ages of 57 – 62, and then he will start with *Es* at 63 for five years (63 – 67). The next letter in Jefferson after *E* is *R*. It takes 9 years to get through *R*, so he would be in *R* from the ages of 68 – 76, but we are only doing his chart through the age of 70. So, for our purposes, just put *Rs* on his Mental/Emotional/Professional Name from 68 – 70, as follows:

Age	58	59	60	61	62	63	64	65	66	67	68	69	70
Physical (1st Name)	I	I	I	I	I	I	A	M	M	M	M	W	W
M/E/P (2nd Name)	F	F	F	F	F	E	E	E	E	E	R	R	R
Spiritual (Last Name)													
Essence													
Personal Year													

Now, we need to complete his Spiritual Name (last name). It takes 33 years to get through Clinton. So, at 66 he will complete Clinton for the second time. Put the last *N* of Clinton at age 66 and work backwards and forwards from there. Remember, it takes five years to get through *N*, so he will be in *N* from the ages of 62 – 66. The letter before the last *N* in Clinton is *O*, and it takes 6 years to get through *O*, so he would be in *O* from the ages of 56 – 61, but our chart is only going back to 58. After he completes the name Clinton at age 66, he will start the name over again at age 67. The letter *C* has a value of 3, so it takes 3 years to get through *C*. The letter following *C* in Clinton is

L (L = 3), so it would take 3 years to get through L. He would be in L from the ages of 70 – 72, but we are abbreviating our chart to end at age 70 for simplicity.

Age	58	59	60	61	62	63	64	65	66	67	68	69	70
Physical (1st Name)	I	I	I	I	I	I	A	M	M	M	M	W	W
M/E/P (2nd Name)	F	F	F	F	F	E	E	E	E	E	R	R	R
Spiritual (Last Name)	O	O	O	O	N	N	N	N	N	C	C	C	L
Essence													
Personal Year													

Now that we have found the letters for each of his names from the ages of 58 – 70, it is time to look for patterns, to calculate the Essence for each year, and to determine what Personal Year he is in at each age. Let's start by drawing a vertical line to separate patterns whenever there is a change. For example, from ages 58 – 61, he is in the pattern *I, F, O*. The pattern changes at age 62 to *I, F, N*, so we would draw a vertical line between ages 61 and 62 to separate the patterns. Do this for other pattern changes as well, as follows on the next page.

Age	58	59	60	61	62	63	64	65	66	67	68	69	70
Physical (1st Name)	I	I	I	I	I	I	A	M	M	M	M	W	W
M/E/P (2nd Name)	F	F	F	F	F	E	E	E	E	E	R	R	R
Spiritual (Last Name)	O	O	O	O	N	N	N	N	N	C	C	C	L
Essence													
Personal Year													

Next, we calculate the Essence for each pattern by adding the value of the letters. For example, at 58 years old, Bill is in the pattern *I, F, O*. The value of *I* = 9, *F* = 6, and *O* = 6. Add and reduce, 9 + 6 + 6 = 21/3. So, from 58 – 61, he is in a 21/3 Essence. Calculate the other patterns by adding the values of their numbers and reducing, if necessary, to get a single digit. The chart with the Essence included will now look as follows on the next page.

Age	58	59	60	61	62	63	64	65	66	67	68	69	70
Physical (1st Name)	I	I	I	I	I	I	A	M	M	M	M	W	W
M/E/P (2nd Name)	F	F	F	F	F	E	E	E	E	E	R	R	R
Spiritual (Last Name)	O	O	O	O	N	N	N	N	N	C	C	C	L
Essence	21/3	21/3	21/3	21/3	20/2	19/ 10/ 1	11/2	14/5	14/5	12/3	16/7	17/8	17/8
Personal Year													

The last calculation we need to do for his chart is the Personal Year Number. Bill was born August 19, 1946, and I'm doing his chart in 2010, so I'll add his birth month, birth day, and the current universal year (2010), then reduce to a single digit. See below:

8+19 (1+9 = 10, 1+0 = 1) + 2010 (2+0+1+0 = 3)
8+1+3 = 12 (1+2 = 3)

So, Bill is in a 3 Personal Year in 2010. Since he is 64 years old as of August 19, 2010, we will put a 3 under the 64. See the completed chart for Bill Clinton from ages 58 – 70 on the next page.

Year	2004	2005	2006	2007	2008	2009	2010	2011	2012	2013	2014	2015	2016
Age	58	59	60	61	62	63	64	65	66	67	68	69	70
Physical (1st Name)	I	I	I	I	I	I	A	M	M	M	M	W	W
M/E/P (2nd Name)	F	F	F	F	F	E	E	E	E	E	R	R	R
Spiritual (Last Name)	O	O	O	O	N	N	N	N	N	C	C	C	L
Essence	21/3	21/3	21/3	21/3	20/2	19/10/1	11/2	14/5	14/5	12/3	16/7	17/8	17/8
Personal Year	6	7	8	9	1	2	3	4	5	6	7	8	9

Now that we have his complete chart, in the next chapter, we'll interpret it.

Chapter 14

Interpreting a Complex Chart

Previously, we determined how William Jefferson Blythe's numbers changed when his name changed to William Jefferson Clinton. Here is a summary of his numbers.

WILLIAM JEFFERSON BLYTHE	WILLIAM JEFFERSON CLINTON
Birth Force Number: 11/2	Birth Force Number: 11/2
Soul Number: 11/2	Soul Number: 14/5
Identity Number: 13/4	Identity Number: 16/7
Impression Number: 24/6	Impression Number: 30/3 or 12/3
Destiny Number: 8	Destiny Number: 23/5

INCLUSION LISTS	
WILLIAM JEFFERSON BLYTHE	**WILLIAM JEFFERSON CLINTON**
1 = 3	1 = 3
2 = 2	2 = 1
3 = 3	3 = 4
4 = 1	4 = 1
5 = 5	5 = 6
6 = 3	6 = 4
7 = 1	7 = 0
8 = 1	8 = 0
9 = 3	9 = 4

If Bill had kept the name Blythe, his numerology chart for this time period would be as follows:

Year	2004	2005	2006	2007	2008	2009	2010	2011	2012	2013	2014	2015	2016
Age	58	59	60	61	62	63	64	65	66	67	68	69	70
Physical (1st Name)	I	I	I	I	I	I	A	M	M	M	M	W	W
M/E/P (2nd Name)	F	F	F	F	F	E	E	E	E	E	R	R	R
Spiritual (Last Name)	L	L	Y	Y	Y	Y	Y	Y	Y	T	T	H	H
Essence	18/9	18/9	22/4	22/4	22/4	21/3	13/4	16/7	16/7	11/2	15/6	22/4	22/4
Personal Year	6	7	8	9	1	2	3	4	5	6	7	8	9

The Blythe chart would differ from the Clinton chart on the spiritual name, and that difference would change his Essence Numbers.

Here is the Clinton chart for that same time period.

Year	2004	2005	2006	2007	2008	2009	2010	2011	2012	2013	2014	2015	2016
Age	58	59	60	61	62	63	64	65	66	67	68	69	70
Physical (1st Name)	I	I	I	I	I	I	A	M	M	M	M	W	W
M/E/P (2nd Name)	F	F	F	F	F	E	E	E	E	E	R	R	R
Spiritual (Last Name)	O	O	O	O	N	N	N	N	N	C	C	C	L
Essence	21/3	21/3	21/3	21/3	20/2	19/10/1	11/2	14/5	14/5	12/3	16/7	17/8	17/8
Personal Year	6	7	8	9	1	2	3	4	5	6	7	8	9

Now, let's extend his chart back to the time that his involvement with Monica Lewinsky came to light. According to Wikipedia (https://en.wikipedia.org/wiki/Monica_Lewinsky), Lewinsky claimed to have had sexual encounters with Clinton between 1995 and 1997, but news of the scandal did not come out until 1998. Let's look at Bill's chart from 1998 to 2004 to see what his numbers show for that time period.

Year	1998	1999	2000	2001	2002	2003	2004
Age	52	53	54	55	56	57	58
Physical (1st Name)	L	L	L	I	I	I	I
M/E/P (2nd Name)	F	F	F	F	F	F	F
Spiritual (Last Name)	N	N	T	T	O	O	O
Essence	14/5	14/5	11/2	17/8	21/3	21/3	21/3
Personal Year	9	1	2	3	4	5	6

At 52 and 53 years old, Bill was in a 14/5 Essence. Remember, 14/5 is a Karmic Number associated with the misuse of personal freedom. This can involve sexual transgressions, chemical imbalances, and/or addictions But, there is more to Bill's karmic story than just his 14/5 Essence Numbers in 1998 and 1999.

Bill Clinton was born William Jefferson Blythe at birth. With his original name, his Inclusion List showed no karmic lessons (he wasn't missing any numbers). When he changed his name to William Jefferson Clinton, he picked up a 14/5 Soul Number. So, with this name (Clinton) he brought the energy of a karmic debt Soul Number and gained another 6 (his original Inclusion List had three 6s, but he added another 6 to the list when he became Clinton). Remember, the number 6 is associated with responsibilities, especially around family. In addition, as Clinton, he is now missing 7s and 8s. These are karmic lessons he must learn as Bill Clinton.

His chart suggests that at 52 and 53 years old – when his 14/5 Essence Number matched his Soul Number – he was paying off a karmic debt. The 14/5 is usually associated with karmic debt that will help you see a path for changing your life and changing your ways.

When we compare his chart with Monica Lewinsky's (DOB: 07/23/1973), we find that she has a 14/5 Birth Force Number that indicates a karmic debt to be repaid. So, his Soul Number came down and matched her Birth Force Number. She had to cross paths with someone with that Karmic Number, and they were working out a past life situation, coming together just long enough to complete what was not completed in a past life.

At 54, he was in an 11/2 Essence and a 2 Personal Year. In the section of this book on Essence Numbers, I told you that I consider the double 2s (2 Essence in a 2 Personal Year) to be the bankruptcy sign. During that time, he likely experienced a significant financial loss.

Age 54 is also when his letters changed on his spiritual name from *N* to *T* (*T* = 2), so he had *T*s at 54 and 55 years old. This major change was dramatic and involved partnerships and relationships. It was like a death of his work, his relationship with his wife, and his reputation with the public.

At 55 years old, his letters on his physical name changed from *L* to *I*. You may recall that the letter *I* is a very emotional letter. He is in the letter *I* on his physical name from 55 – 63 years old, and stress and negative emotions may have adversely affected his health during that time.

At age 56, Bill experienced another change. The letters on his spiritual name changed from *T* to *O* and put him in a 21/3 Essence. If you refer again to the Clinton chart that we created for him from the ages of 58 – 70, you'll see that he remained in that 21/3 Essence from 56 – 61 years old. Whereas the 12/3 Essence is a time of being a free spirit, the 21/3 Essence is a time of feeling restricted. So, from 56 – 61 years old, he likely felt as if his hands were tied and like he was no longer in control of anything.

In addition to the 21/3 Essence that began in 2002 at age 56, he was also in a 13/4 Personal Year (his birth month and day + the calendar year, so 8+19/10/1+2002 = 13/4). A 13/4 Personal Year is dramatic and often involves the loss of friendships and relationships, job, and home. This makes sense for Bill given his presidency ended in 2001.

Despite these challenges, the letter O in his chart on his spiritual name from 56 – 61 years old suggests that his loved ones in the Spirit world were protecting him.

In 2008, at the age of 62, he was in a 20/2 Essence. At 63 years old he was in a 2 Personal Year, and at 64 he was in an 11/2 Essence. You may remember that a 2 over a 2 (e.g., a 2 Essence in a 2 Personal Year) can be an indication of a bankruptcy. He was not in a 2 over a 2, but from 2008 – 2010, he had the 2 Essence, 2 Personal Year, and then 2 Essence again, suggesting that he was on the cusp of having to rebuild his finances, and he was dealing with financial matters going on around him.

In 2009, at age 63, he was challenged to rise from the lower self (19/10/1) and to find acceptance with all that had happened.

In 2010, when he was 64 years old, he had an A on his physical name, suggesting an important physical change, such as a move or a need to watch his health. Remember, when you see an A, circle it, as this is an indication of an important change.

Even though Bill changed his name to Clinton, he will still have the Blythe influence. His Identity Number as Blythe is 13/4, and on the Blythe chart, he was in a 13/4 Essence in 2010. So, he may have experienced an identity crisis at that time.

From 65 – 66 years old, he was back in the 14/5 Essence paying off more karma. At 67, when his letters changed on his spiritual name from N to C, he likely felt happier than he had felt in many years. Remember, Cs are associated with happiness, socializing, and caring. He was in a 6 Personal Year, a time involving responsibilities, especially regarding family. His Essence Number changed to a 12/3, suggesting that he felt freer than he had in many years.

The year 2014, when he was 68, had the potential to be significant in terms of paying off karma. To understand why, let's review his karmic debts and lessons again.

With his name change to Clinton, his physical name and his mental/emotional/professional names did not change. So, he still has to face and deal with those. The spiritual is what changed with the name change to Clinton.

When he was Blythe, the consonants on his physical name (William) and on his spiritual name (Blythe) were both 15/6, indicating that he was very balanced. He paid off a debt on his spiritual name when he became Clinton. The 15/6 from the consonants in Blythe was paid off. I say this because the vowels in Clinton equal 15/6, and vowels represent our past lives. So, the 15/6 of Blythe went to the past when he became Clinton.

However, taking the name Clinton gave him an imbalance with the physical in this lifetime, and it gave him the Karmic Soul Number 14/5. The name change gave him karmic lessons too, because now he is missing two numbers in his Inclusion List – the numbers 7 (introspection) and 8 (finances).

Bill's Identity Number also changed when he became Clinton. It became a 16/7, and that is also a Karmic Number. The Karmic Number 16/7 warns of losses in this lifetime. The losses may manifest as tragedies, disgrace, loss of power or fortune, or deception in relationships. The 16/7 involves a cycle of destruction and rebuilding of one's life. Satisfying this debt requires learning the spiritual truths involving willpower and what is right. And that is exactly what Bill had the opportunity to do in 2014, at age 68.

Although Bill has no 7s in his Inclusion List, he was in a double 7 (16/7 Essence in a 7 Personal Year) at age 68. And with his 16/7 Identity Number, this was a time for him to pay off significant karmic debt and come into his true life and his true identity.

At 69, he had a double 8 (17/8 Essence in an 8 Personal Year), so he may have been more active in politics and in better shape financially at that time.

Conclusion

When choosing a numerology chart to include as an example, I decided upon Bill Clinton's chart because of its complexity. If you were able to follow this example and understand my interpretation, you will likely have little difficulty in creating and interpreting your own chart and the charts of others.

One final note...I have mentioned that Spirit will direct me to see certain things in the chart and will guide me in the interpretation. If you are a medium or a student of mediumship who wishes to use my system of numerology as a tool in your readings, work with your spirit guides on how best to incorporate this tool.

If you are not a medium, but you wish to develop mediumship abilities, I encourage you to take classes and get involved in a spiritual development circle. There are wonderful Spiritualist centers in the United States including Camp Chesterfield in Indiana, Lily Dale in New York, and Cassadaga, Florida, among others. You can contact the National Spiritualist Association of Churches for more information.

References

Balliett, Mrs. L. Dow. 1905. *How to Attain Success Though the Strength of Vibration: A System of Numbers as Taught by Pythagoras.* London: L.N. Fowler & Co.

Wikipedia. 2014. "Bill Clinton: Early Life and Career." Last modified November 17, 2014. https://en.wikipedia.org/wiki/Bill_Clinton

Wikipedia. 2014. "Monica Lewinsky: Scandal." Last modified November 12, 2014. https://en.wikipedia.org/wiki/Monica_Lewinsky

Wikipedia. 2014. "Barack Obama: Early Life and Career." Last modified November 12, 2014. http://en.wikipedia.org/wiki/Barack_Obama#Early_life_and_career